Curiosities

of

West Midlands

Curiosities

of

West Midlands

A County Guide
to the Unusual

by

Julie Meech

S.B. Publications

To Nicholas -
because he said he'd be interested in this one.

First published in 1993 by S. B. Publications
c/o 19, Grove Road, Seaford, East Sussex, BN25 1TP

ISBN 1 85770 038 4

Typeset, printed and bound by Manchester Free Press,
Longford Trading Estate, Thomas Street, Stretford, Manchester, M32 0JT. tel: 061-864 4540

CONTENTS

CONTENTS

CONTENTS

Front cover: Section of Snow Hill Mural, Birmingham

Back Cover: Delph Ninelocks, Brierley Hill

Half title page: Scene from "Alice in Smerick", Smethwick

ACKNOWLEDGEMENTS

Thanks are due to the following:-

Nora Watts and Audrey Wells at Hampton in Arden, for welcoming me, my muddy shoes and my tripod into the church they'd just finished cleaning. Thanks especially to Nora for taking the time to point out so much which I would have missed otherwise.

Michael, security guard at the Jewellery Business Centre.

Roger, in the pro department at Jessop Photo Centre on New Street.

Sandwell Metropolitan Borough Council's Department of Technical Services, for producing such first class interpretative material about the borough's heritage.

All those people who write and illustrate the useful booklets available in most churches.

Steve, for extending the deadline!

INTRODUCTION

West Midlands is a polygenous county of two and a half million people with different traditions, loyalties, attitudes and accents. It was cobbled together in 1974 with chunks snatched fron Staffordshire, Warwickshire and Worcestershire - and few were impressed by the process. Even the name was ill-chosen; West Midlands, we had all thought, meant that region comprising Herefordshire, Shropshire, Staffordshire, Warwickshire and Worcestershire. Confusion reigned, and still does. Nearly twenty years later there are still those who refer to the county as **the** West Midlands. It's hardly surprising.

Confusion aside, local identity is so strong that each distinct area has managed to hold on to it. Woe betide you if you call a Black Countryman a Brummie, or vice versa. And it could even be argued that there was a certain logic in the creation for there is one unifying theme which runs through it - industry. From Wolverhampton in the north-west, to Coventry in the south-east, industry is basically what the county is about, though there is, it is true, a small area of green belt, hardly countryside.

In the eighteenth and nineteenth centuries this was the industrial heartland not merely of England, but of the world. And since those early days of industrialisation when green fields became "dark satanic mills" almost overnight, the region has been constantly renewing itself. Small forges and workshops were replaced by huge brick factories which were replaced by fabricated sheds. Cottages were replaced by terraces which were replaced by tower blocks. Rutted, muddy roads were sidelined by canals which were superseded by railways which were overshadowed by motorways. Now the latest twist has canals and industrial premises being spruced up for a new generation of leisure users; collieries and quarries being turned into parks and nature reserves.

Over two centuries of such change, coupled with massive war-time destruction at Coventry, sets the tone for this book which must embrace the word "curiosity" in its widest sense. What may be commonplace elsewhere can easily assume curiosity value here. How, for instance, does a thirteenth-century manor house manage to survive just a short distance from the M5/M6 interchange? The legacy of the Industrial Revolution has its own fascination. In an age of mass production we can marvel at the loving care which once went into designing a humble little canal bridge. Modern additions to the landscape tend to be less satisfying, but some of them do, at least, emphasise that this part of the world is still at the forefront of technological advance.

On a practical note - map references have been given for the Birmingham A-Z which covers the whole county. If you prefer to use OS Landrangers the relevant ones are 139 and 140. The best way to get around is by public transport; unlike rural counties West Midlands still has excellent services. With two exceptions (Temple Balsall and the Crooked House) nothing in this book is more than a minute's walk from the nearest bus stop. Many are close to railway stations. However, prospective train users should take note of one extra little "curiosity" supplied by British Rail - Sandwell and Dudley Station is not at Sandwell and it's not at Dudley; it's at Oldbury!

I hope you will use this book as a starting point to get to know the county better. It may not be the most picturesque of English shires, but it has character. I think you will find it grows on you.

Julie Meech

BIRMINGHAM — CITY CENTRE

CATHEDRAL OF ST PHILIP: NANETTA'S GRAVE

Access: St Philip's is between Colmore Row and Temple Row; Nanetta's grave is close to the main entrance. A-Z 73 3H

Work began on St Philip's in 1711 and it was consecrated in 1715. The architect was Thomas Archer, the builder William Shakespeare, and the dedication to St Philip owed nothing whatsoever to the saint, but was inspired by Robert Phillips of Warwick who donated the land on which it was built!

Archer chose the Baroque style for his church, and it is often considered one of the best buildings of its type in the country. Impressive it undoubtedly is, and well worth a visit, but compared to most cathedrals it lacks interest. Perhaps this is due to its comparatively recent date; or maybe it's because it was built as a parish church, becoming a cathedral only in 1905 when the new Diocese of Birmingham was created.

There are some imposing gravestones around the cathedral but one of the most interesting is also one of the most easily missed. No more than a yard long, it marks the final resting place of Nanetta Stocker who died in 1810. At only 33" tall, Nanetta is described as "the smallest woman ever in this kingdom" but one who was, nevertheless, "possessed with every accomplishment".

BIRMINGHAM — CITY CENTRE

THE ANGEL DRINKING FOUNTAIN

> *Access:* On Temple Row, on the edge of St Philip's churchyard. A-Z 73 3H

This cast iron drinking fountain is set into pedimented stonework in a fairly prominent position on the edge of St Philip's graveyard, and yet, perhaps because it's so dark in colour, and is no longer in use, it's all too easy to walk past it without even seeing it. This is a pity because it's an unusual and delightful piece of work which deserves to be better known.

The fountain originally stood outside Christ Church at the junction of Colmore Row and New Street. Although the church was only consecrated in 1813 a declining city centre population led to its demolition in 1899 and the angel was moved to her present position.

Her book displays the text "Whosoever drinketh of this water shall thirst again but whosoever drinketh of the water I shall give shall never thirst".

BIRMINGHAM — CITY CENTRE

THE TOWN HALL

Access: In Chamberlain Square. A-Z 73 3H

Birmingham Town Hall was designed by Joseph Hansom, whose previous work included Beaumaris Jail, and who was later to find fame as the inventor of the Hansom Cab. Faced in Anglesey marble, and based on the Temple of Castor and Pollux in Rome, it incorporates a Corinthian colonnade of 42 columns 30' high. The interior is equally impressive.

Unfortunately, the terms of his contract were such that Hansom soon found himself in financial trouble and was declared bankrupt in 1834. Local architect Charles Edge took over, finally completing the work several years later. Today, the Town Hall serves mainly as a concert venue and has a long and distinguished musical history. Mendelssohn conducted here in 1837 and 1846, Elgar's "Dream of Gerontius" had its first performance, and in 1912 Sibelius conducted his "Fourth Symphony".

Less peacefully, the Town Hall was the scene of riots in 1901 on the occasion of a speech by the pro-Boer Lloyd George. The fact that the Brummies' beloved MP Joe Chamberlain was anti-Boer was enough to anger the mob and those who had tickets stormed the stage while those outside hurled bricks through the windows and took a battering ram to the doors, chanting "We'll throw Lloyd George in the fountain and he won't come to Brum no more." Lloyd George escaped only by swapping clothes with a policeman, the crowd failing to recognise the diminutive figure in the over- large uniform. The mob eventually dispersed, but not before one man had died in the crush.

BIRMINGHAM — CITY CENTRE

79–83 COLMORE ROW: TWO FLORENTINE CRAFTSMEN

Access: Colmore Row runs from Chamberlain Square to Colmore Circus Queensway. A-Z 73 3H

Colmore Row was remodelled by the Victorians from 1866 onwards to reflect the increasing prosperity and status of the city. Though its integrity has been compromised by later developments it still boasts a number of fine buildings worth more than a cursory glance. The three-storey edifice at 79–83, now occupied by the Royal Bank of Scotland, is not only well proportioned and ornate, but also has two interesting roundels, one on either side of the third-storey row of windows. These depict the heads of Benvenuto Cellini and Lorenzo Ghiberti, and although they are veiled by pigeon netting they still catch the eye.

But what do these two Italians have to do with Birmingham? Nothing really, but the explanation lies in the fact that 79-83 was built for a Mr Spurrier, silversmith and cutler, who chose to use its façade to commemorate two rather more famous craftsmen.

Ghiberti lived from 1378 to 1455, and the bronze doors he created at the Baptistry in Florence were described by Michelangelo as fit for the gates of Paradise. The design of the Colmore Row roundels is said to bear some similarity to a series of Heads of the Prophets on the east door of the Baptistry.

Cellini, who lived from 1500 to 1571, is perhaps the most renowned goldsmith of all time, although his most famous work, also in Florence, is a bronze statue of Perseus with the head of Medusa. He was also a writer and his autobiography revealed much about the time he lived in.

Colmore Row and the streets around it, Bennett's Hill for instance, contain a number of other interesting details well above street level and the whole area repays leisurely exploration.

The Roundels at 79–83 Colmore Row

BIRMINGHAM — CITY CENTRE

A CANAL CROSSROADS

> *Access*: At Old Turn Junction, also known as Deep Cutting Junction, between the National Indoor Arena and the International Convention Centre.
> A-Z 73 3G

It is often said, and correctly so, that Birmingham has more miles of canal than Venice. Furthermore, the city is at the heart of a navigation system which extends to over 4,000 miles throughout Britain. From Birmingham you can travel by boat to the Irish Sea, the North Sea, the Thames estuary or the Bristol Channel. At Old Turn Junction, where three major canals converge in the city centre, is a "traffic island", topped by a signpost, which can be regarded as the crossroads of the entire British canal system. The three which meet here are the Birmingham Canal Navigation Main Line, the Birmingham and Fazeley and the Worcester and Birmingham. The signpost indicates Wolverhampton, Worcester and Fazeley, with distances in miles and the number of locks.

The island is of World War Two construction. The former London, Midland and Scottish railway line to Wolverhampton runs beneath the canal at this point; a direct hit by German bombs would have sent thousands of gallons of water flooding into the tunnel. Engineers designed safety gates to close against the island under sudden water pressure to prevent flooding.

BIRMINGHAM — CITY CENTRE

CURZON STREET GOODS STATION

Access: On the corner of Curzon Street and New Canal Street. A-Z 74 3B

Completed in 1838, Curzon Street Station was designed by architect Philip Hardwick as a counterpart to Euston at the other end of the line. Sadly, Euston's imposing Doric portico was demolished in the brutal 1960's, despite much public protest. By some fortunate chance Curzon Street's equally imposing Ionic portico still survives.

A squarish, three-storey building, it has four massive fluted columns 50' high, splendid carvings above the entrance and balustraded windows on the first floor. Originally, this tremendous façade opened onto an equally impressive booking hall; today it gives access only to a goods yard, the status to which Curzon Street was relegated as early as 1854 when New Street Station replaced it as a more central terminus for passengers from London. That early New Street Station was also a fine building but has itself been superseded by a modern version, even more relentlessly unattractive than its counterpart at Euston. The entrance to Curzon Street Goods Yard is all that remains in Birmingham of the architectural splendours of the golden age of the railways.

BIRMINGHAM — CITY CENTRE

THE BIRMINGHAM GUN-BARREL PROOF HOUSE

Access: On Banbury Street near Curzon Street Goods Station. A-Z 74 3B

Although the gun trade was established early on in Birmingham it was not until the reign of William III that the town first became pre-eminent. But, before long, Birmingham gunmakers were the Army's leading suppliers and by 1767 there were 62 gun workshops. Together they were exporting thousands of guns every week and then came the Napoleonic Wars and such an expansion in trade that Birmingham became known as the gunshop of the world.

Guns require testing before use and in 1813 a special Act of Parliament gave Birmingham the right to its own proving authority. It was with great pride that the town saw the opening of the Proof House in March 1814.

Approached through an interesting gateway, the building is of mellow brick and classical design, by John Horton of nearby Deritend. Above the entrance is a striking, vividly-coloured plaster coat of arms by local sculptor William Hollins, featuring weapons, drums, uniforms and flags.

Under the Gun-Barrel Proof Acts every gun sold in the UK or exported abroad must be tested at the Proof House and marked with the now world-famous stamp of a crown over crossed sceptres. At its peak the Proof House was testing 900,000 guns a year; numbers are now nearer 50,000 but the method is unchanged. The gun is simply overcharged and fired; if all goes well it is passed, if it blows up it has failed.

You can view the exterior from 8am Mondays-Fridays - or see it from the train as you approach New Street. To visit the small museum inside first telephone 021 643 3860

BIRMINGHAM — CITY CENTRE

CHURCH OF ST THOMAS

> *Access:* On Bath Row near Five Ways. A-Z 73 4H

There is not a great deal left of St Thomas's but what there is looks very impressive, if oddly truncated. The church was built 1826-9 in the Greek revival style, from attractive golden stone, with two fine Ionic curved colonnades and a central arch beneath a graceful tower. Designed by Thomas Rickman and Henry Hutchinson it was, despite its grand appearance, intended merely as a chapel in the parish of St Martin's, Birmingham's mother church.

The present incomplete appearance is due to enemy bombs and so it is fitting that a Peace Garden, sponsored by the City Council, and partly financed by the European Regional Development Fund, has been created behind its remains. The garden is enclosed by railings which incorporate an unusual design featuring a variety of animals, including man. Along the north side is a colonnaded loggia of white stone, whose walls, along with those of the church, bear a number of plaques inscribed with messages on the theme of peace. They represent a variety of faiths, everything from Humanism to Hinduism, and numerous cities and nations around the world. It will depend on your viewpoint whether you find the message from the people of Yugoslavia poignant or simply ironic, but others such as an extract from Lawrence Robert Binyon's "Eulogy to the Fallen", are undoubtedly moving. Most intriguing, however, is the message from a Nairobi safari company - see if you can work out what it means!

BIRMINGHAM — CITY CENTRE

THE OLD SQUARE MURAL

> *Access:* Old Square is at the north end of Corporation Street, below the
> Queensway ringroad. A-Z 74 3A

Old Square is today a dismal little shopping precinct at the meeting place of
several subways under Priory Queensway. But it was not always so, and a relief
mural, designed by Kenneth Budd and Associates, tells the story of the square's
history, revealing a long and interesting past.

In the early Middle Ages an Augustinian priory stood here - hence Priory
Queensway. The site later came into secular ownership under the de
Berminghams, and the square itself, one of elegant and imposing town houses,
was built in 1713. For the next century or more a good many prominent citizens
made their homes here, but it gradually changed into a commercial centre and, by
1896, the last of the original houses had been demolished.

Among the former residents of Old Square featured in the mural are Sampson
Lloyd and Samuel Galton. Lloyd (more correctly Llwyd) was a Welsh Quaker who
could trace his ancestry back many centuries to a distant King of Dyfed. He came
to Birmingham to make his fortune and, with a colleague, he founded Taylor's
and Lloyd's Bank. He lived at number thirteen Old Square in 1770, and is
commemorated in the mural by a beehive - the early motif of today's "black horse
bank".

There must have been something about number thirteen because, ten years later,
another notable man was living there. Samuel Galton had many claims to fame
but the mural celebrates his involvement with the Lunar Society, an organisation
which came into being around 1776. Its members were wealthy, educated,
prominent men - industrialists, scientists, doctors, artists and writers - who met at
each other's homes for intellectual discussion; men such as Matthew Boulton,
James Watt, William Withering, Erasmus Darwin and Josiah Wedgwood. The
name "lunar" refers not to their mental health, but to their habit of meeting on the
Monday nearest the full moon so that, in those days of unlit streets, they would
have light to guide them home. To Samuel Galton's butler, however, and, no
doubt, to many of his contemporaries, they were the "lunaticks"(18th-century
spelling as used by Galton's butler).

Details from the Old Square Mural

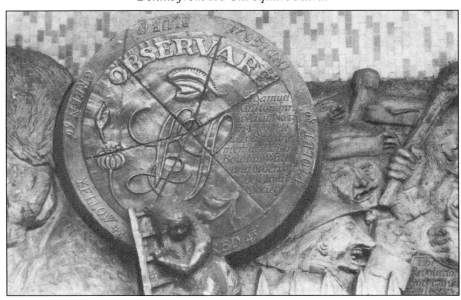

BIRMINGHAM — CITY CENTRE

SNOW HILL MURAL: REMEMBERING THE GWR

> *Access:* In the gardens by the subway entrances below St Chad's Circus on Snow Hill, close to the railway station. A-Z 73 2H

When Birmingham suffered the disastrous redevelopments of the 1960's some attempt was made to humanise the pedestrian concrete warrens running under the city by adding a series of murals, most of which detail aspects of local history. There are several of these dotted around - or rather, beneath - the city centre, but the semi-circular one below St Chad's Circus is particularly striking. At 300' by 17' it is one of the largest murals in the world and it tells the story of the Great Western Railway's route from London to Snow Hill Station, the construction of which began in 1847. Made from a mosaic of small pieces of coloured tile, the mural also incorporates the openings of two subways into the design as the portals of railway tunnels.

Designed by Kenneth Budd and Alan Kemp, and completed in 1969, the mural involved a team of researchers in six months' work at Swindon Railway Museum in an effort to get every last detail of the locos and the rolling stock absolutely right.

Inset panels tell the story in words, but not so vividly as the pictures which include details such as Dash, the station dog at the turn of the century, and a pair of characters who look suspiciously like Sherlock Holmes and Dr Watson on their way to solving some hideous murder.

I K Brunel was the engineer in charge of construction and by 1852 the 129-mile track from Paddington was completed. Snow Hill Station opened the same year and a special eve-of-opening train left London the previous day, pulled by "The Lord of the Isles", which had been on show at the Great Exhibition at Crystal Palace. The "Lord" was derailed at Aynho but the train completed the journey the following day after a change of engine. Plus ça change...

In 1967 the last-ever express left Paddington for Snow Hill but the station continued to handle local trains until 1972 when it was closed. In 1987, however, a new local station was opened on the same site.

Fans of the GWR should also take a look at the now blocked-up station entrance on Livery Street, in the shadow of a multi-storey car park.

Snow Hill Mural

BIRMINGHAM — CITY CENTRE

JEWELLERY BUSINESS CENTRE

Access: On Spenser Street, Hockley. A-Z 73 2G

In Hockley is to be found Birmingham's famous Jewellery Quarter, a commercial asset which this enterprising city has also managed to turn into a rather unlikely tourist attraction. The jewellery trade is a venerable one in Birmingham with its roots in the fifteenth century. It was not, however, until the eighteenth century that the trade began to assume national, and even international, importance. Though the trade has declined from its peak in the early twentieth century, when 30,000 people earned a living in this way, Birmingham is still world-famous for its gold- and silver-smithing and the Quarter is home to over 250 jewellers and smiths, as well as the Birmingham School of Jewellery, a new Discovery Centre for tourists, and the Jewellery Business Centre.

The latter represents the continuing importance of the ancient trade in the life of

the modern city. It was designed for use by the jewellery industry and related businesses in an inner city regeneration scheme created by the Prince of Wales through the Duchy of Cornwall. The Centre has been provided with massive and extremely striking gates commissioned by the Duchy in 1991 from sculptor Michael Johnson. They are largely symbolic, working on several different levels; at its simplest the design is a metaphorical tree of life, but it also represents base metals growing into fine jewels and, although the size and strength of the gates demonstrate the security of the Business Centre, one is left permanently open to provide a welcome. The gates are crafted from stainless steel, cast brass and glass, representing silver, gold and precious stones.

BIRMINGHAM — CITY CENTRE

R J TURLEY

Access: On Warstone Lane, Hockley. A-Z 73 2G

The Jewellery Quarter covers a large area and contains numerous architectural gems. Some of the premises were purpose built, others converted from gracious Georgian town houses; some housed a single operation, others several, or even dozens. There is a great deal to see and a whole book could easily be devoted to the Quarter; indeed, at least two have already been written. Apart from its intrinsic and architectural interest the Quarter is one of the most important surviving examples of the transition from an essentially domestic to a mainly industrialised economy, yet one where the domestic element does still linger on.

It's difficult to pick out individual examples from such a wide choice but R J Turley's is a worthy contender. The shop is particularly eye-catching thanks to the oversized replica wedding ring above the door, rather like an unusual pub sign. Look through the windows and it's like being transported back to the 1880's. One window opens into the showroom where the walls are wood-panelled with a tiled dado rail, the floor is of brick, brass scales sit on the counter and, in winter, a fire blazes in a cast iron fireplace with tiled surround, under a mantlepiece adorned by Staffordshire china dogs. The other window gives a view of the workroom with its characteristic scalloped workbench, made from solid elm and littered with the traditional tools of the trade, all still in daily use for Turley's is a thriving business, not a museum piece.

BIRMINGHAM — CITY CENTRE

THE ARGENT WORKS

Access: At the junction of Frederick Street and Graham Street, Hockley. A-Z 73 3G

At the opposite end of the scale from R J Turley's is the huge and distinctive Argent Works, built in 1862 in a colourful, castellated Italianate style with corner towers. It was intended as a factory for the making of gold pens and pencils, and employed around 250 people. The owner ingeniously found a second use for the building by cashing in on the steam produced by the factory boilers - he opened a Turkish Bath, an attraction popularised in Britain by troops returning from the Crimea. A contemporary newspaper reported on the great luxury of the fittings, which included Indian rugs and soft couches. Billiards, chess, fencing and other amusements were provided; in fact "nothing has been omitted that could add to the enjoyment of the bathers".

The works was constructed using an unusual technique which employed hollow bricks through which iron rods were threaded to increase strength and fire resistance.

More highlights of the Jewellery Quarter are to be found in Charlotte Street, Vittoria Street, Vyse Street, Caroline Street and others. Don't miss the Victoria Works on Graham Street, the " jewellers' church" in St Paul's Square, or the pelican adorning the former Pelican Works on Great Hampton Street.

BIRMINGHAM — CITY CENTRE

THE CHAMBERLAIN CLOCK-TOWER

Access: At the Warstone Lane/Vyse Street/Frederick Street crossroads, Hockley. A-Z 73 2G

This green-painted, cast iron clock-tower is to be found in the Jewellery Quarter, in the heart of what was Joe Chamberlain's constituency, and was erected in 1903 to commemorate his two- month conciliatory visit to South Africa after the Boer War. He was welcomed back to Birmingham by torchlight processions and the clock-tower, made at the nearby Soho Clock Factory, was put in place soon after.

Such adulation for a politician may seem misplaced but Chamberlain, who was Birmingham's Mayor from 1873 to 1876, and later represented it in Parliament, set out to improve and transform the city with unprecedented vigour and enthusiasm. He gave Birmingham an almost unparalleled municipal pride and confidence and, in return, its citizens gave him their loyalty and admiration. A more substantial memorial to him, also built during his lifetime, is the monumental fountain in Chamberlain Square near the Town Hall.

BIRMINGHAM — CITY CENTRE

THE WAR STONE

> *Access:* On Warstone Lane, Hockley. A-Z 73 2G

Despite the obvious connotation there is nothing bellicose about the War Stone, as the inscription on its plinth makes clear:-

> *This felsite boulder was deposited near here by a glacier during the Ice Age, being at one time used as a parish boundary mark it was known as the Hoar Stone of which the modern War Stone is a corruption.*

Felsite is a type of amorphous rock and many such boulders, technically known as erratics, were left behind in the West Midlands as the glacier retreated at the end of the last Ice Age some 10,000 years ago. Others have given their names to Great Stone Road in Northfield and Gilbertsone Road in Yardley.

The word "hoar" has other meanings today but in medieval England it was applied to stones used as markers on boundary lines. The word has survived uncorrupted in Hoar Cross (Staffordshire) and Hoarwithy (Herefordshire).

18

BIRMINGHAM — CITY CENTRE

WARSTONE LANE CEMETERY AND KEY HILL CEMETERY

Access: From Warstone Lane and Icknield Street. A-Z 73 2G

These two Victorian cemeteries are only yards apart and both are of interest. Warstone Lane contains many jewellers' graves, including those of the splendidly named Ensor Trouts who, oddly enough, are buried almost opposite the Salmons. An unusual but dominant theme among the memorials is a rather ugly tree motif, often entwined with ivy and sometimes in the shape of a cross. In the middle of the cemetery are terraced stone catacombs.

Key Hill is an altogether more melancholy and evocative place, especially after the trees have shed their leaves in autumn. On one side are towering sandstone cliffs, on top of which teeter abandoned industrial workshops. The cliffs are unexpected but the explanation is that this was once a quarry supplying sand for use in iron working. Once exhausted, the site was turned into a cemetery, laid out around a Doric temple, now gone. It also had a look-out post so that a watch could be kept for body-snatchers, all too prevalent in the days when fresh corpses for dissection fetched good prices from unscrupulous doctors. There are extensive catacombs, their entrances closed by huge inscribed doors commemorating the families sealed within.

The cemetery contains the graves of a number of Birmingham notables, such as John Baskerville the printer, and it was here that Joseph Chamberlain's ashes were scattered in 1914.

On a more prosaic note, one of the city's famous "iron conveniences" can be found in the north-west corner.

BIRMINGHAM — CITY CENTRE

A CAST IRON URINAL

Access: On Vyse Street, Hockley. A-Z 73 2G

In its industrial heyday Birmingham achieved fame for its distinctive wrought and cast iron work, producing, for instance, decorative gates and clock-towers as well as more mundane artefacts such as urinals. Mundane or not, they were meant to be decorative as well as functional and were given elaborate designs. Very often, they were attached to the exterior walls of back street pubs and Birmingham became known as the "Home of the Iron Convenience". A number still survive to enhance the street scene today. This one is on Vyse Street, near the Jewellery Quarter, but you can see others (and use them, too, if you're a man) at the corner of New Canal Street and Fazeley Street, on Lancaster Street, Banbury Street and Coventry Road. There is a disused one in a dreadfully dingy situation under the railway bridge on Allison Street and another disused one built into a railway bridge on Livery Street. They are painted in different colours but mostly in rather sombre shades of blue, grey, olive etc.

BOURNVILLE

THE GARDEN VILLAGE

Access: The area around Cadburys' factory, which is on the A4040 and next to Bournville Station. A-Z 104/5 1D/E

Arrive at Bournville by train and you step out onto a station painted in those rich shades of purple and gold so familiar to all chocoholics. Next to it is the factory, bordered by playing fields, and beyond these is Bournville Green, the heart of the garden village founded by the Cadbury brothers over 100 years ago.

It was in 1879 that George and Richard Cadbury moved the family business from the city to what was then leafy Worcestershire. The Cadburys, especially George, wanted to provide better conditions for their workers, but there were also sound business reasons for the move and the valley of the Bourn Brook, with its proximity to both railway and canal, was well chosen. The new community was named Bournville, as this was thought to have a French ring to it, French chocolate then being highly prized.

Some houses were built immediately, but it wasn't until 1893 that George Cadbury set about creating his model village. From the start it was a success and has continued to grow ever since, administered by the Bournville Village Trust. Not all the houses are reserved for Cadburys' workers so it has not become a kind of company ghetto.

Bournville is a hugely attractive suburb but the area around the factory remains the most interesting. At the centre of the Green stands an octagonal brick rest house, modelled on the yarn market in Dunster, Somerset, and given as a Silver Wedding Present in 1914 to George and Elizabeth Cadbury by their workforce. Opposite it stands another particularly notable building, the Junior School, its clock-tower surmounted by a cupola and an unusual carillon of 48 bells.

Bournville Green - The Rest House

Bournville - Selly Manor

BOURNVILLE

SELLY MANOR AND MINWORTH GREAVES

> *Access:* On the corner of Maple Road and Sycamore Road, next to Bournville Green. A-Z 105 1E

Although Bournville was built after 1879 it contains two much older timber-framed houses which now constitute Selly Manor Museum. Selly Manor itself dates back to at least the 1320's and originally stood about a mile away. When threatened with demolition it was bought by George Cadbury, dismantled and re-erected on its present site. It's a beautiful building which has been well restored; particularly notable is the two-storey porch over an exterior staircase to the first floor. The Manor was opened to the public in 1917 and houses the impressive Laurence Cadbury Collection of vernacular furniture.

Next door is Minworth Greaves, thought to be almost 750 years old. It was rescued from Curdworth, north of the city, where it had stood in a state of decay for about 40 years. It was in such poor condition that only the main timbers could be saved, but these included some splendid cruck beams. Cruck construction was an early technique and comparatively few cruck-framed buildings survive. Each pair of crucks was usually hewn from a single tree split in half, giving rise to the characteristic curved shape of such timbers.

Selly Manor Museum is open Tuesdays-Fridays (tel. 021 472 0199). There are many more interesting buildings in Bournville, and lots of green spaces. A new attraction at the factory itself is Cadbury World, a museum devoted to the story of chocolate; everything from the Aztecs to the dashing Milk Tray hero.

EDGBASTON

PERROTT'S FOLLY

> *Access:*   On Waterworks Road, off Monument Road, Ladywood. A-Z 73 4E

Also known as The Monument, and billed as "Birmingham's most eccentric building" by the charity that owns it, this unusual tower was built in 1758 by local landowner John Perrott on his country estate Rotton Park. Seven storeys, or 96' high, the folly is an octagonal, brick tower with battlements and Gothic windows. Inside, a spiral staircase with 139 steps gives access to the upper floors which house various displays and a tearoom. On the top floor is an ornate drawing room and from the roof there are extensive views.

In 1884 the tower was leased by the Midland Institute as an observatory and became one of the world's first weather recording and forecasting stations, continuing in that capacity for nearly 100 years. By 1984 it was in poor condition and the Perrott's Folly Company was set up to purchase and renovate it.

But what was its purpose in the first place? Various theories have been advanced, some rather more bizarre than the folly itself. One suggestion is that Perrott wanted to watch over his wife's grave - but this was several miles away with some substantial buildings blocking the view. Only slightly less unlikely is the idea that he wished to check on the activities of his lover in her home at Five Ways. But maybe Perrott merely enjoyed looking out over what was then countryside or, perhaps, in an age when follies were the height of fashion, he was simply keeping up with the Joneses.

You can view the tower at any time but the interior is open only from 2 to 5 on Sundays and Bank Holiday Mondays from Easter to September.

EDGBASTON

CHURCH OF ST BARTHOLOMEW: A NUMERICAL PUZZLE

> *Access:* On Church Road, at its junction with Priory Road, next to Edgbaston
> Park Golf Course, just west of the A38 Bristol Road. A-Z 89 1G

St Bartholomew's was plundered by the Roundheads in 1644, with the lead from the roof being melted down into bullets and the timbers used to barricade Edgbaston Hall, captured from its Royalist owner Richard Middlemore. This led to extensive reconstruction after the Interregnum, followed by further work in the nineteenth century, so that today very little survives of the original medieval building. Nonetheless, St Bartholomew's remains a handsome church well worth a visit.

It contains what has, so far, proved an unsolvable mystery - above the north door is carved what appears to be the number 777. What this means nobody knows, but it probably dates to the post- Cromwellian reconstruction, and two possible explanations have been offered; firstly that it represents the date of the original chapel, remembered in folk history; secondly, that it is actually derived from a letter rather than a number - M for Middlemore. Perhaps a mason, faced with a badly eroded medieval M, deciphered it instead as 777 and carved what he thought was a suitable replacement.

Of the two theories, perhaps the second is the more likely, or maybe both are wide of the mark. The only thing that seems certain is that we shall never know.

EDGBASTON

CHURCH OF ST BARTHOLOMEW: THE WITHERING MEMORIAL

St Bartholomew's contains some fine memorials, including one to Dr William Withering who once lived at Edgbaston Hall. He died in 1799 and is buried in the church. His memorial, carved in 1808 by William Hollins, features a snake twined around a twig, and two plants, one of which is easily recognisable as a foxglove (digitalis purpurea). This is to commemorate Withering's discovery of the drug digitalis; but perhaps "discovery" is the wrong word, for Withering became aware of the foxglove's powers only when a Shropshire gypsy used an infusion of foxglove leaves to cure a patient whom the doctor had thought a hopeless case.

So impressed was he that he spent months searching for the gypsy before he finally found him again and was able to obtain the details of the infusion. He published the gypsy's knowledge in "An Account of the Foxglove and some of its Medicinal Uses" in 1785 and it became a classic of medical literature, giving a full account of the use of digitalis in the treatment of heart disease. The drug remains in use today.

Withering was also, with Dr John Ash, a founder of Birmingham General Hospital, and a distinguished member of the Lunar Society.

HALL GREEN

SAREHOLE MILL

Access: On Cole Bank Road, a short distance west of the A34 Stratford Road. A-Z 91 5E

Sarehole Mill stands beside the River Cole in a small green enclave in suburbia. As the last water mill to survive in Birmingham it is now administered as a museum by the City Council. There must have been a mill on the site for many centuries but the present buildings are mainly Georgian, having been rebuilt in the 1760's when the corn mill was adapted to grind metal, thus playing a small part in the Industrial Revolution. For a time it was leased by James Watt's partner Matthew Boulton. The mill later reverted to more pastoral use, again grinding corn and also bone, and was last used commercially in 1919, after which it fell into disrepair. It was restored to working order in the 1960's.

Whether seen as a picturesque rural survivor, as a small player in the Industrial Revolution, or as a memorial to Matthew Boulton, the mill is obviously of great value. But there is another dimension to it, less well known yet for many of us more potent. For the last four years of the nineteenth century Sarehole Mill and the surrounding woods and meadows were the playground of John Ronald Reuel Tolkien, and it was Sarehole which was in his mind when he created "The Shire", the home of Bilbo, Frodo and Sam, heroes of "The Hobbit" and "The Lord of the Rings" which, between them, have sold over 55 million copies.

Tolkien was born in South Africa in 1892 but his father was originally from Birmingham and his mother from Evesham. In 1895 Mrs Tolkien brought her two boys, John and Hilary, back to England for a holiday. Her husband died while they were away and she decided not to return to Africa. In 1896 she rented 264 Wake Green Road in what was then the village of Sarehole. The village has been engulfed by the suburbs of Hall Green and Moseley but the house is still there, just around the corner from the mill.

The family lived there for only four years, but the young Tolkien had brought with him hot, dry, dusty memories of the veldt and this new experience of meadows, trees and water made a deep and lasting impression on him. Years later, in 1966, he told journalist John Ezard "It was a kind of lost paradise...I loved it with an intensity..."

In Tolkien's day the mill was operated by a Mr Andrew and his son George. The brothers nicknamed George "the white ogre" as he was usually covered in bone dust when he chased them out of his yard. "The two of them were perishing little nuisances" recalled George Andrew in 1959. The feeling was mutual and the millers in Tolkien's books are surly characters.

But trouble with the neighbours didn't diminish Tolkien's love of Sarehole and although the family moved closer to Birmingham in 1900 he never forgot his early years in the country. If Birmingham was later to inspire the "black land of Mordor" Sarehole, though now much changed, is also immortalised as the hobbits' idyllic "Shire".

Sarehole Mill

KING'S NORTON

THE OLD GRAMMAR SCHOOL

> *Access:* In a corner of the churchyard on The Green, off the A441 Pershore Road
> South. A-Z 105 5E

With its large gardens and tree-filled park, King's Norton is a pleasant place, and
on The Green there still survives a small enclave of the past, consisting of the
fourteenth century church, the Saracen's Head and the Old Grammar School. The
Grammar School is one of the oldest in the Midlands. The timber-framed upper
storey, supported on pillars, was built in the early fifteenth century; the brick
ground floor, on stone foundations, was underbuilt in the Elizabethan period.

A plaque above the door records that Thomas Hall "Schoolmaster Preacher
Bibliophile" taught here from 1629 to 1667. Hall was only nineteen when
appointed but soon gained such a reputation for his teaching skills that pupils
were sent to him from all over the country. He was less popular with local
people, many of whom found themselves out of tune with his austere
Presbyterianism.

He was a prolific writer who came up with titles such as "The loathsomeness of
long hair" and "Painting of spots and naked breasts . . . to inflame lusts in the
hearts of Men". Brilliant teacher he may have been, but school was obviously not
a whole lot of fun for his pupils.

In later years the school declined and fell into disuse. In the early twentieth
century it was sold for £10 to Theodore Pritchett who gave it to the church. In
1951 it was restored with the help of a grant from the Pilgrim Trust and is now
used by the choir.

KING'S NORTON

THE SARACEN'S HEAD

> *Access:*   Next to the churchyard on The Green.

On the south side of St Nicholas's churchyard is the former Saracen's Head, a jettied, timber-framed building of unblackened oak which probably started life as the principal residence of the Manor about 800 years ago, in the days when King's Norton far outranked Birmingham in importance. (Local tradition insists that even as recently as two centuries ago letters would be addressed to "Birmingham, near King's Norton"). Much of the present fabric of the building is late fifteenth century and it may have been around this time that it first became an inn. It is thought that in the sixteenth and seventeenth centuries it was used as a trading centre by local wool merchants, and it has had a variety of other uses over the years. It was, for a time, the residence of the Royal Bailiff and Henrietta Maria spent a night here in the 1640's; travelling with a fair sized army, which camped around the village, she was on her way to join her husband Charles I. In the late nineteenth and early twentieth centuries it served as a grocer's, a chemist's and a tea-room. In 1930 Mitchells and Butlers gave it to the parish and it became a community centre and later the parish office. In 1972 a trust was set up for future restoration work and much still needs to be done.

KING'S NORTON

GUILLOTINE LOCK

> *Access:* On the Stratford Canal below Lifford Lane/Broadmeadow Lane Bridge.
> A-Z 105 4F

Not only is King's Norton greener and leafier than most Birmingham suburbs, it also has the benefit of two canals - the Worcester and Birmingham and the Stratford-on-Avon. At their junction stands a very attractive former toll house and 200 yards further on, over the Stratford Canal, is a most unusual guillotine stop lock.

The Stratford Canal was built in the days when rival canal companies were possessive about their water supplies; this guillotine lock was constructed to prevent the flow of water from the Stratford to the Worcester. There are two guillotines, a boat's length apart; each consists of wooden gates mounted in iron frames and balanced by chains and counterweights. The normal position was with the gates lowered, but on the approach of a boat the nearer gate was raised to allow the vessel entry, then lowered behind it. The same procedure was repeated with the second guillotine, thus ensuring that no water was lost to the rival canal. Since nationalisation in 1948 the guillotines have remained permanently open.

Adjacent to the lock are some mill ponds where ducks swim contentedly outside the former papermill which now houses the Patrick Motor Museum. When the mill was working it relied on coal transported along the canal system from Smethwick.

MOSELEY

MOSELEY HALL DOVECOTE

Access: In the grounds of Moseley Hall Hospital on Alcester Road (A435)
A-Z 90 4A

Moseley is one of the pleasanter Birmingham suburbs and it is not that many years since much of it was still farmland. The land now occupied by Moseley Hall Hospital was formerly part of the estate of Moseley Hall, a timber-framed farmhouse occupied by the Grevis family from the fifteenth century to the eighteenth.

There were also two subsidiary farms on the estate and one of these, South Farm, was close to the present hospital entrance. South Farm's dovecote, an octagonal, red-brick structure three storeys high, still survives, along with the much-altered remains of a former forage store known as the Cowhouse.

Probably built at the beginning of the eighteenth century, the dovecote later fell into disuse although pigs were sometimes housed on its ground floor. In 1933 it was decided to pull down all the South Farm buildings but, after a campaign by local people, the dovecote was spared. It was greatly dilapidated and plans were drawn up for its restoration but it was actually 1981 before work finally started.

The dovecote, now in excellent shape, belongs to the Central Birmingham Health Authority but is maintained by the Moseley Society. You can see the exterior from the road but the interior, which contains some interesting displays, is open only on the first Saturday of each summer month from 2.30 to 5 - these times are subject to change so do check first.

NORTHFIELD

THE VILLAGE POUND AND THE GREAT STONE

Access: On Church Road, opposite St Lawrence's church. A-Z 104 4A

Like King's Norton, Northfield is frequently described as having retained much of its village character. This is optimistic, to say the least, but the heart of the former village is still a pleasant and rather unexpected place, with brick cottages bordering a green below a handsome church.

Opposite St Lawrence's is the Great Stone pub and, adjoining it, a sandstone pound with a heavy wood and iron gate. Most villages had a pound at one time in order to confine stray cattle for confiscation, but only a handful now survive. This seventeenth century one is not only rare but also one of the finest there is, and the only real reminder that, until comparatively recently, Northfield was an agricultural village. Even in the 1850's there were still 52 farms in the parish; there are none today, the last having gone under concrete and tarmac in the 1960's.

Inside the pound is the Great Stone, which has given its name both to the pub and to nearby Great Stone Road. This is another of Birmingham's erratics - boulders carried down, probably from North Wales, by advancing ice sheets, and left behind as the ice retreated. It used to stand on the corner of Church Road and Church Hill but was moved the few yards to its present position in the 1950's.

The pub is allegedly a late medieval timber-framed hall house encased in eighteenth century brick. It has been known to make the claim that its beer is "sold by the stone".

BRIERLEY HILL

DELPH NINELOCKS

Access: Between Delph Road and Mill Street. A-Z 68 4A

Delph Ninelocks is a spectacular piece of canal engineering, but "ninelocks" is a misnomer for there are only eight. Just to add to the confusion, an adjacent pub is named The Tenth Lock. All this, however, is not merely an example of the famous Black Country humour; there were, in fact, nine locks once and the old name has stuck.

The name Delph derives from a former description of the area, Black Delve, which refers to the numerous collieries once worked here. The orginal canal was built in 1799, with nine locks on this section enabling the waterway to climb from the 350' level of the Stourbridge Canal to the 441' of the Dudley Number One. The coal workings, however, caused subsidence which affected the locks and in 1856 it was decided to rebuild the flight. The original top and bottom locks were retained but the remaining seven were replaced by only six new ones which took a more direct course up the hill. Parts of the original system were retained as overflow weirs.

Close to the top is a stable block once used to house the boat horses, and, at the very top, is a fine Horseley Ironworks cast iron roving bridge spanning the original course of the canal.

Ninelocks is surrounded by areas of grassland, woodland and wetland where birds, butterflies and wild flowers all flourish - a tiny green oasis just hundreds of yards from the madness and mayhem of Merry Hill.

BRIERLEY HILL

THE VINE

<table>
<tr><td>Access: On Delph Road. A-Z 68 4A</td></tr>
</table>

The old narrowboatmen reputedly had prodigious thirsts - which is one reason why the Black Country, with its extensive canal network, has so many pubs. Nowhere is this more obvious than in the area around Brierley Hill and it is here, close to Delph Ninelocks, that you will find the Vine, better known locally as the Bull and Bladder. Widely considered the best of all the Black Country pubs (though fans of the Swan at Netherton would have something to say about that) it is a magnet for committed beer drinkers who appreciate its atmosphere and, more especially, its home-brewed ale, made at the adjoining Batham's Brewery.

Daniel Batham and Sons supply just eight tied houses, although a handful of free houses also sell the famous brew which has helped to make the Black Country the real ale centre of Britain. In 1991 Batham's Best Bitter was pronounced Britain's Champion Bitter by CAMRA. The quote from "The Two Gentlemen of Verona" on the pub's façade sums it up - "BLESSING OF YOUR HEART: YOU BREW GOOD ALE"

BRIERLEY HILL

THE MONORAIL

> *Access:*   At Merry Hill Centre. A-Z 68 3B

Merry Hill was once the site of the famous Round Oak Steelworks which was in production for nearly two centuries until closed down in 1983. Today it's the 200 acre Merry Hill Shopping Centre, christened Merry Hell by some unconvinced locals; a huge complex of over 260 shops spread over 2½ miles of covered malls. There is parking for 10,000 cars and on the edge of the site are the usual retail sheds. As if this weren't terrifying enough, there's more still at the planning stage.

For those shoppers who don't fancy the trek across the car park, from M&S to Texas for instance, there's a solution at hand - what is proudly described as "the most futuristic transport system in the northern hemisphere" can whisk you smoothly from shop to shed in seconds. It's an electric monorail which glides noiselessly over 1¼ miles of overhead dual track between, would you believe, Times Square, Central Station and Waterfront East! There are four "trains" altogether and each can carry 150 passengers at 3½ minute intervals.

Wouldn't it be good to see such impressive technology put to real use in providing efficient public transport in our car-clogged cities? To be fair, a rapid transit system (at street level) is planned for West Midlands, but it hasn't happened yet. In the meantime, if you're wondering why this is claimed to be the most futuristic transport system only in the northern hemisphere, that's because there's one down under in Sydney.

DUDLEY

THE SPOUT

Access: In the market place. A-Z 55 3E

The Spout is the local name for an unusually grand fountain in the centre of Dudley's attractive and lively market place. It was commissioned by the Earl of Dudley and sculpted by James Forsyth, who was also responsible for the famous Poseidon fountain at Witley Court, Lord Dudley's Worcestershire home. The Spout was considered splendid enough to be displayed at the Paris Exhibition in 1867 before being installed in its present position, where it was unveiled by the

Countess of Dudley. It's an elaborate affair of Italian Renaissance design; yet the fruits and flowers carved upon it are appropriate enough for its market place setting, and somehow even its exuberant horses, lions and dolphins don't seem out of place.

The fountain was declared "the property of the people of Dudley forever", and attempts to move it into a local park, out of the way of increasing traffic, were foiled by public protest. Happily, the market place has since been pedestrianised and the Spout is safe for the foreseeable future.

DUDLEY

THE WREN'S NEST

> *Access:* Fron Wren's Hill Road, Cedar Road, Bluebell Park etc. North-west of the town centre. A-Z 54 1C 1D 2D

Imagine, if you can, a time when Dudley was a coral reef washed by clear tropical seas! It may take a prodigious leap of the imagination but, after all, it was a long time ago - some 400 million years in fact, in what is now known as the Silurian era. Yet certain inhabitants of tropical Dudley, such as sea scorpions, sea lilies and trilobites, can still be found in the modern town at the Wren's Nest, a 74 acre outcrop of Wenlock limestone known to locals as the Wrenner.

The Wrenner was subject to mining and quarrying in the eighteenth and nineteenth centuries, and so many fossils were found that Dudley achieved international fame in geological circles. The most frequent find was a species of trilobite, Calymene blumenbachi, which was so numerous that it became known as the Dudley Bug and was incorporated into the town's coat of arms. Dudley Bugs are found in collections all over the world, but some of the best are in the geological gallery at the town's own museum.

The collecting mania of the Victorians led to three fossil shops being established in Dudley and today the site is largely denuded, although some fossils may be seen in the loose material below the main rock faces. But there's more to the Wrenner than fossils and it's worth a visit just for the interest of its exposed limestone strata which is most striking on the western side of the outcrop, while on the eastern side a chain of underground canals and quarry workings has been exposed by rock falls. The site was declared a National Nature Reserve in 1956, mainly for its geological importance, but naturalists will also find plenty of interest. Kestrels nest on the rock face and foxes patrol the woodland which clothes the lower slopes.

The Wren's Nest

GORNALWOOD

THE CROOKED HOUSE

> *Access:* Down a lane off the B4176 Himley Road just west of Gornalwood.
> A-Z 53 3E

Strictly speaking, the Crooked House is probably in Staffordshire, but if so it's by a matter of inches and in character it belongs to the Black Country - most of which was, of course, previously in Staffordshire anyway.

Although now best known as the Crooked House, this pub used to be the Glynne Arms, and in local dialect it's still the Siden House to some. Thanks to subsidence in this former coal-mining area the pub leans at a crazy angle, its southern end propped up by heavy buttresses. Presumably, it's not unusual to feel slightly dizzy on leaving a pub, but at this one you feel dizzy on entry as you walk through the outer door which leans sharply in one direction, only to be confronted by an inner door leaning just as sharply in the other. It's almost enough to make you seasick and, once inside, you'll find wall-clocks, lights and curtains which all appear to hang at an angle, while a marble or coin placed on the "lower" end of a table will roll uphill.

Perhaps Gornalwood is an appropriate place for the Crooked House, for together with its neighbours, Upper and Lower Gornal, it has traditionally been the butt of Black Country humour. The story is told, for instance, of two windmills built at nearby Ruiton - and the subsequent dismantling of one of them when Gornal folk realised there was insufficient wind for both!

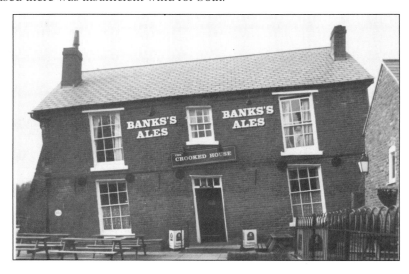

NETHERTON

WINDMILL END

Access: In Warren's Hall Park, by the Dudley Canal south-east of Netherton, between the A459 Halesowen Road and the B4171 Dudley Road. A-Z 69 2F

A one-time quarrying and coal-mining centre, Netherton was also important for ironworking industries, particularly nail-making. Consequently, the canal system was also a major part of its story and Windmill End is the site of a canal junction beneath the colliery- and quarry-scarred Rowley Hills.

The collieries in this area were plagued by water penetration which had to be dealt with by pumping and so Cobb's Engine House, named after a local farmer, was built here in 1831. The red brick building housed a beam engine which took water from the mines and discharged it into a local watercourse and later, after its construction, into the Netherton Tunnel Branch Canal. By the 1920's most mines in the area had ceased production and Cobb's was one of the last pumping houses to shut down in 1928. The engine was scrapped and all that remains now is the engine house with its adjacent 95' chimney stack. Although only a shell it is probably the earliest of its type still in existence, and is a Grade II Listed Building and a Scheduled Ancient Monument.

The surrounding pits and spoil heaps have been grassed over and landscaped. Trees and ponds, together with the canals, constitute a valuable wildlife habitat and this is one of the best places in the Black Country to see swans and even kingfishers.

The canals are crossed by three striking, black and white, cast iron roving bridges made at the Toll End works, and the south portal to Netherton Tunnel is here too. Built in 1858, the tunnel runs 3,027 yards to Dudley Port and was remarkable in its day for its width which allows towpaths on either side. It was also lit throughout by gas lamps - today you'll need a torch, and its light will reveal strange limestone formations on the brickwork, caused by water seepage through the overlying rock.

A short walk to the west brings you to the appealingly-named Bumble Hole Basin and, back at Windmill End, you'll find the Dry Dock, a Little Pub Company property where the bar is a narrowboat and a notice on the wall advises you to "Beware of the cat".

In 1991 Windmill End was the venue for the Black Country National Waterways Festival and it's hard to imagine a better setting for such an event

Windmill End - Cobb's Engine House and the Dry Dock

SMETHWICK

THE OLD AND NEW MAIN LINES AND THE NEW PUMPING STATION

> *Access:* From Brasshouse Lane Bridge near Smethwick Rolfe Street Station. A-Z 58 5A

Smethwick contains perhaps the greatest concentration of canal engineering and architecture in Britain, with major works by Brindley, Smeaton and Telford. In recognition of this, Sandwell Metropolitan Borough Council has created the Galton Valley Canal Heritage Area and excellent leaflets about this can be obtained from Smethwick Library.

Two canals run side by side below Brasshouse Lane Bridge and you can trace the course of a third. The first to be built was Brindley's 1760's contour canal which followed a meandering course between Birmingham and Wolverhampton. It was bedevilled by water shortages and congestion and was replaced by Smeaton's Old Main Line in 1790. Brindley's canal has gone but the footpath on the north side of the cutting runs at the same level. Before long, Smeaton's canal also proved inadequate and Telford pronounced it "little better than a crooked ditch". His New Main Line, an engineering masterpiece, was opened in 1829.

Between the two is the New Pumping Station, a late addition to the canal scene, not being completed until 1892. A large, squarish building, with a tall chimney in alternating bands of blue and red brick, it is a commanding presence in the deep cutting. It was built to replace James Watt's nearby Smethwick Engine of 1779 which is now in Birmingham Museum of Science and Industry. It had the capacity to lift 200 lockfuls of water from the New Main Line to the higher Old Main Line, counteracting water loss as boats passed through the locks. But the canal age was already past its heyday and the pumping station was closed in the 1920's and allowed to decay until restoration began in 1982.

SMETHWICK

GALTON BRIDGE

> *Access:* From Roebuck Lane, off the A457 Oldbury Road and close to Smethwick
> West Station. A-Z 57 5H

Thomas Telford began his working life as a humble apprentice mason and
became the greatest engineer of the late eighteenth and early nineteenth
centuries. His New Main Line of the Birmingham canal abounds in engineering
masterpieces, but perhaps the greatest is the combination of the Galton Bridge
with the Smethwick Summit cutting.

The bridge, light and elegant in design, soars 71' above the canal at the deepest
part of the cutting. With a span of 150' it was, at the time of its construction, the
world's largest single span bridge, crossing the world's largest earthwork. A
contemporary writer described the New Main Line as "unsurpassed in stupendous
magnificence by any similar work in the world". It's easy to smile at such
nineteenth century hyperbole today - until you remember that every cubic inch of
soil that was removed to make the cut was removed, not by men with JCBs,
cranes and bulldozers, but by men with picks, shovels and wheel barrows.
Looked at in that light, any superlatives seem less than adequate.

The bridge, a Grade One Listed Building, was cast at Horseley Ironworks, and
named after Samuel Galton, Chairman of the Birmingham Canal Company's
Finance Committee in 1826 and a prominent member of the Lunar Society. It was
put in place to take a road across the cutting but today it carries only a footpath,
the road having been superseded by a new dual carriageway which has been
named Telford Way. The irony of such an intended tribute is that Telford Way has
destroyed for ever the view of Telford's bridge from the west, depriving it of the
setting it once had and still deserves.

SMETHWICK

ENGINE ARM AQUEDUCT

> *Access:* From Brasshouse Lane or Bridge Street, near Smethwick Rolfe Street Station. A-Z 58 5A

The Engine Arm Aqueduct is another of Telford's masterpieces, built in 1825 as part of his improvements to the Birmingham Canal. Cast at Horseley Ironworks in Tipton, it consists of a trough supported by an arch with stone piers at either end. The arch includes an elaborate tracery of Gothic detailing which gives it almost a medieval and ecclesiastical look. A scheduled Ancient Monument, it was restored in 1985, a colourful paint scheme making the most of the fine detail of the ironwork.

The care and attention to detail which went into the design, making it beautiful as well as functional, is all the more remarkable when you consider that its purpose was merely to carry an unimportant branch canal across the New Main Line, 20' below. The Engine Arm was a feeder from Rotton Park Reservoir to the Old Main Line at Smethwick Summit and was also used to convey coal to the engine on Bridge Street from which it took its name. Smethwick Engine, designed by James Watt, was built to pump water from the bottom lock to the Summit. It operated from 1779 until 1892 when it was replaced by the New Smethwick Pumping Station. Although not the first engine built by Watt, it is the oldest surviving one, and is now in Birmingham Museum of Science and Industry where it is steamed regularly. Its site on Bridge Street has recently been excavated and also scheduled as an Ancient Monument.

SMETHWICK

THE TOLL HOUSE AND "ALICE IN SMERICK"

Access: On the High Street. A-Z 58 1A

This listed building, a two-storey stucco cottage, which stands on Smethwick's busy modern High Street, was built in 1818 for the collection of tolls on the Birmingham, Dudley and Wolverhampton Turnpike, which opened in 1760. Originally, the Toll House had blue gates, which explains why both the pub and the market opposite are called "Blue Gates".

On the front you can see the recess which would have formerly contained the toll board, sadly now missing. The Toll House was restored in 1983 under the Galton Valley Canal Park scheme run jointly by West Midlands County Council and Sandwell Metropolitan Borough Council. It currently houses information about the arts in Smethwick, particularly the superb contemporary mural "Alice in Smerick" (only **very** loosely based on "Alice in Wonderland"!) which, in sixteen colourful panels, adorns the adjoining wall separating the High Street from the A457 Tollhouse Way.

The Toll House, Smethwick

Scene from "Alice in Smerick"

STOURBRIDGE

THE BONDED STORES

> *Access:* On Canal Street, west of the A491 Amblecote High Street and just north
> of Stourbridge town centre. A-Z 83 1F

The Bonded Stores is a warehouse situated on the Stourbridge Canal's Town Arm,
a branch extending just over a mile from Wordsley Junction to its terminus at the
Amblecote end of Stourbridge. An unusual, three-storey brick building, its upper
floors supported by cast iron columns, the Stores was built in 1779, extended in
1849, and recently restored. It now serves as a base for the Stourbridge
Navigation Trust and as a community centre where local societies may meet.
Across the street are the former offices of the Stourbridge Canal Company, and
moorings for narrowboats extend along the arm, making this a colourful and
interesting corner of the town. A little further along is the historic Stourbridge
Ironworks where the "Stourbridge Lion", the first steam locomotive to run in
America, and the "Agenoria," the first in the Midlands, were built in 1829.

If you would like to see inside the warehouse it's open by arrangement;
telephone 0384 395216. Public boat trips operate from here in the summer.

TIPTON

THE PIE FACTORY

> *Access:* At the corner of Hurst Lane and Sedgley Road. A-Z 43 5E

"A pub? A restaurant? A museum? Or just a joke?" So asks Sandwell Council in one of its promotional leaflets - and concludes that the only answer is to go and judge for yourself. And so you should, for no exploration of the Black Country is complete without a visit to the Pie Factory, one of a chain belonging to the Little Pub Company, owned by Mad O'Rourke, whose real name is rumoured to be Colum, and whose motto is "Unspoilt by Breweries".

Each pub is built around a different theme, such as The Dry Dock by the canal at Windmill End and The Sausage Works at Cradley, and they have achieved a sort of cult status. At The Pie Factory cow pie, also known as Dan pie (after Desperate Dan of *Beano* fame) is the

speciality, and it comes complete with pastry horns, as illustrated on the pub's façade. If you've got the stamina, and you're not concerned about cholesterol overload, you can follow your Dan pie with a pudding such as spotted dick, and wash it all down with a pint of Lumphammer ale.

Although Black Country based, the Little Pub Company is branching out, with the Sauce Factory at Worcester and the Muggery at Upton-on-Severn. It's rumoured that Mad is on the verge of expanding nationally, but what Southerners will make of his pubs is anybody's guess!

WEDNESBURY

CHURCH OF ST BARTHOLOMEW: THE FIGHTING COCK

Access: On Church Hill, off Walsall Street. A-Z 44 1D

Wednesbury - Woden's burg - is an ancient place and there are some who believe that there was once a temple to the Norse god Woden on the site where St Bartholomew's now stands. The present church is mainly fifteenth century, though of earlier origin, and from the outside its blackened stone makes for a rather forbidding appearance. The interior, however, is beautiful and houses a number of treasures.

Foremost amongst these is a unique lectern which, instead of the traditional eagle, features a proud fighting cock grasping an oak pedestal with his sharp talons. Believed to be fourteenth century, the cock is made of wood with a beautifully gilded finish.

It has been suggested that the lectern was installed by a nineteenth century vicar with a most unchristian passion for cockfighting, but as it predates the nineteenth century by so many years this seems unlikely. It probably reflects the widespread local interest in this barbarous "sport" which, though banned at the end of the eighteenth century, actually continued for another hundred years or so. Neighbouring towns may have been just as heavily involved but an eighteenth century ballad called "Wednesbury Cocking" has helped to link this town in particular with the so-called "sport".

Close to the lectern is a superb Jacobean pulpit and you should not miss a fourteenth century chest dug up in the graveyard, the alabaster Parkes monument and a priceless painting of 1698 once dismissed as a "bundle of rubbish".

WEST BROMWICH

OAK HOUSE

> *Access:* On Oak Road, ¹/₂ mile from the High Street via Lodge Road. A-Z 57 3E

The Oak House is a remarkable survivor - a gabled, timber-framed building marooned in a sea of Victorian terraces in an area brutally transformed by the Industrial Revolution. One of the finest buildings of its kind in the Midlands, Oak House was constructed of massive oak beams joined in the post and truss method. The oldest parts are the central hall and the side wings which date from the reign of Henry VIII in the earlier sixteenth century. The lantern tower was added some time in the seventeenth century and is a very rare feature. It is sometimes suggested that it was used as an observation tower during the Civil War but other experts think it is of slightly later construction. Whenever it was built, it's a delightful addition to the house.

The earliest recorded occupants of Oak House were the Turtons who moved here in 1634. They were originally from Lancashire and had made their money in nailmaking, an industry which was later to assume great importance in the Black Country.

By 1894 the house had fallen into disrepair and was purchased by Alderman Reuben Farley who paid for its restoration and presented it to the town for use as a museum. It underwent further restoration after World War Two and was reopened in 1951. Many of its rooms are panelled and it contains a fine collection of sixteenth and seventeenth century furniture. Outside are pleasant gardens where John Wesley preached in 1774.

The Oak House is open to the public most days; for details ring 021 553 0759. You can admire the exterior at any time.

WEST BROMWICH

THE MANOR HOUSE

Access: On Hall Green Road just west of the A4031 Walsall Road. A-Z 45 3F

The Manor House is an unexpected find in an area of inter-war suburban housing close to the M6. Its position is odd in another sense too, for although it is the original Manor of West Bromwich it is actually closer to Wednesbury. This is due to the focus of West Bromwich moving south in the last century. In fact, the present High Street was unenclosed common land until 1804.

The decline of the Manor House dates from around the same time and it was eventually converted into tenements housing several families. Encased in brick and plaster, there was no clue as to what lay behind the façade and its history was forgotten. By 1950 the building appeared to be derelict and was purchased by West Bromwich Corporation for the purpose of demolition. However, expert investigation resulted in the discovery that beneath the crumbling plaster lay one of the most unspoilt examples of a medieval manor house in England, complete with great hall, solar crosswings, kitchen block, chapel and gatehouse.

A full restoration was carried out, followed by further refurbishments twenty years later. The moat, long filled in, was redug and supplied with water and the grounds were landscaped. In 1987 the application of dendrochronology (tree-ring dating) indicated that the timber for the great hall had been felled in 1275.

The Manor House functions as a pub and restaurant, open during normal licensing hours. The grounds are open from dawn to dusk. A small museum of items found on the site is housed in the chapel.

WORDSLEY

THE RED HOUSE CONE

> *Access:* At the corner of Camp Hill and Bridge Street. A-Z 67 4E

Thanks to abundant sand and coal, and good quality fireclay, the Stourbridge area has been renowned for glassmaking for at least 400 years, and even today it's one of the most important local industries. But manufacturing methods have changed and the cone- shaped furnaces which were once a common sight have disappeared, with the exception of that still standing at Red House Glassworks, one of only four left in Britain. Superficially, it resembles the pottery cones of Staffordshire, but those were simply ovens whereas the glass cone was a workshop too.

90' high and 60' in diameter at the base, the Red House cone was built of brick in 1790 and last used for commercial production in 1936. Some of the adjacent factory buildings are contemporary with the cone, others were added later. Since 1881 the site has belonged to Stuart and Sons which now produces its famous crystal at a modern factory across the road and has restored the old site to form a fascinating museum.

The cone used to house a central furnace around which the glassmakers worked. The peripheral area was also used for various purposes and coal was fed into the furnace by men working in tunnels. Although smoke and fumes were meant to escape through a hole at the top of the cone, and the doors were left open, it must, nevertheless, have been an uncomfortable working environment.

Walk along Bridge Street and you can view the glassworks in the context of the canal which provided the means of transporting the finished items. A flight of locks here, the Stourbridge Sixteen, takes the canal 148' up the hill towards Dudley, and is also known as the Staircase because of the brief distance between each lock. There are old iron split bridges (to allow the passage of the towrope), a side pond much favoured by moorhens, and a basin with an unusual timber warehouse known as Dadford's Shed after the canal engineer Thomas Dadford.

Red House Cone

COVENTRY — CITY CENTRE

ST MARY'S HALL

Access: On Bayley Lane, south of the cathedrals. A-Z 116 5B

One of the finest Medieval guildhalls in the country, St Mary's was built in 1340-2 for the newly established Merchant Guild, and was enlarged in 1400 for the Trinity Guild, although it is also thought to incorporate the remains of a twelfth century castle belonging to the Earls of Chester. Its street frontage is sandstone and, with its tower and great arched window, it resembles an ecclesiastical building, but there is a timber- framed courtyard and much magnificent timber-work inside.

St Mary's is open to the public in summer and you can explore most of the rooms inside, which include a council chamber, complete with an impressive guild chair of 1450, and a treasury, entered through a massive wooden door with three locks; all three keyholders had to be present before access was possible.

Most important is the Great Hall, 30' by 75', which has a very fine panelled and bossed roof and a minstrels' gallery, but is especially noted for its north wall in which a huge, stained glass window of around 1500 casts light on a unique wall-hung tapestry which features a religious scene together with the kneeling figure of Henry VII and Elizabeth, his Queen. The tapestry was probably made for a visit by the Royal couple in 1500 when they were made Brother and Sister of Trinity Guild. The great window above is the one visible from the street and it features a number of notable English kings including Richard I, Henry V, William I and Edward III.

Henry and Elizabeth were probably not the first Royal visitors to St Mary's for the Black Prince was Lord of the Manor of Cheylesmore and most likely attended guild banquets here around 1360. In Elizabeth's time the guildhall served briefly as a prison for Mary, Queen of Scots.

Its fortunes declined over the years and it was used, at times, as both a fish market and a soup kitchen. Election riots in the eighteenth century caused some damage, and German bombs in 1941 considerably more. Skilful restoration has been necessary to present the superb building we see today.

St Mary's Hall

COVENTRY — CITY CENTRE

CHURCH OF THE HOLY TRINITY: THE DOOM PAINTING

Access: On Trinity Street. A-Z 116 4B

Holy Trinity was founded in 1043 by Leofric and Godiva but the present building dates from the thirteenth century and has been heavily restored since. It contains one of the finest Medieval wall paintings in England; it's above the arch facing you as you walk in. You can't see much of it though, for the Doom Painting, as it is called, is largely hidden beneath a layer of grime. Although its existence has been known for a long time it was assumed that it was in poor condition, and it was only in 1986 that workmen checking the electric wiring discovered that, beneath the dirt, the painting is almost pristine. Restoration poses a dilemma, however, because the plaster is fixed to the stonework by badly decayed timber battens; any disturbance could result in both battens and plaster crumbling, thus destroying the painting forever.

From the ground, you can only really make out Christ's head, which is in the centre. Closer inspection, however, has revealed a wealth of detail. The subject is the Last Judgement - hence Doom Painting - and it's thought to date from the fifteenth century. Christ sits on a rainbow surrounded by Apostles, the Virgin Mary and corpses climbing out of their coffins. Also featured are the Heavenly City, St John the Baptist, the damned and devils issuing from the flames of Hell. If, and when, a way is found to safely restore the mural, it will be a magnificent sight.

There is much else to see in Holy Trinity, and it's interesting to note that there was once a public right of way under the south transept; the archway which formerly gave access to it may still be seen (see St Matthew's, Walsall).

COVENTRY — CITY CENTRE

FORD'S HOSPITAL

> *Access:*   On Greyfriars Lane which runs south from the High Street/Broadgate
> junction. A-Z 116 5B

Founded in 1509, the "hospital" (used in the sense of almshouses) was named
after William Ford, a Coventry merchant who bequeathed the money for its
foundation. Built around a narrow courtyard, it is one of the finest and most
charming examples of timber-framed architecture in Britain. Unfortunately, it was
badly damaged during the air raids of November 1940 and eight lives were lost.
After the war, it was skilfully restored, using most of the original timbers, and in
1966 it was modernised to provide seven flats, each with kitchen and bathroom,
for the inmates, as well as an extra flat for a warden.

Today the residents are all
elderly ladies but in 1509
William Ford directed that it
was to be for five men and one
woman. Ford's executor,
William Pisford, enlarged the
hospital to offer homes to six
men and their wives. Each
couple was provided with
sevenpence-halfpenny a week.

More changes followed when
William Wigston decided that
there was room for only five
couples, together with a
resident nurse and a "pious,
poor woman . . . to superintend
these five poor men and their
wives". This same William also
decided that when a man was
widowed he would continue to
receive the whole sevenpence-
halfpenny; but if the husband
died first the wife would
receive only half this amount!

You may view the exterior at
any reasonable time but the
interior is private.

COVENTRY — CITY CENTRE

CHURCH OF ST JOHN THE BAPTIST

> *Access:* On Fleet Street. A-Z 116 4A

St John's Church was founded in 1344 on land given by Queen Isabella, the widow of Edward II, but there have been several renovations since this time. During the late seventeenth century it fell into disuse and was taken over by a textile manufacturer as a stretch yard. A house-to-house collection was made in 1726 to pay for repairs and further work was necessary in 1858, 1900 and after the last war when the church was badly damaged in air raids. Despite all this restoration work St John's is still a building of great interest. It has an imposing central tower with battlements and overhanging turrets, common enough in Medieval castles but most unusual in a church. The interior is beautiful but strangely constructed, with no two walls parallel and no corner a perfect right-angle.

St John's is also known as the Bablake Church, after Babbelak, the name of the piece of land given by the Queen. It was at first a collegiate church and gave its name to the adjoining Bablake School.

During the Civil War Coventry was a staunch Parliamentary stronghold and St John's Church was used to imprison Royalists captured elsewhere in the Midlands. A contemporary document referred to these troops who had been "sent to Coventry" and, because the townsfolk shunned them completely, a now familiar phrase was born.

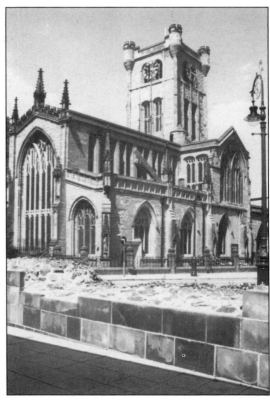

COVENTRY — CITY CENTRE

BABLAKE OLD SCHOOL

> *Access:* On Hill Street, next to St John's Church. A-Z 116 4A

Forming an attractive group with Bond's Hospital, Bablake Old School is built on the site of collegiate buildings of St John's Church, which were established in 1344. The present building is, however, the result of an extensive remodelling in 1560, and came about as the result of a strange but fortuitous error. Thomas Wheatley, a Mayor of Coventry, and also an iron merchant, ordered some iron bars and received silver instead. He waited for it to be reclaimed but heard nothing and finally sold the silver, using the profit to rebuild the college which he named Bablake Hospital. The idea was to provide a home for 21 poor boys, and a nurse to care for them. The boys would be fed, clothed and educated before taking up apprenticeships. It later became an ordinary boys' school and remained as such until 1890 when the school transferred to new buildings in Coundon Road. Bablake later became a museum and is now used as offices.

COVENTRY — CITY CENTRE

BOND'S HOSPITAL

Access: On Hill Street, next to St John's Church. A-Z 116 4A

Thomas Bond was Mayor of Coventry in 1497, and in 1506 a hospital or almshouse was established on this site by the terms of his will. The hospital provided for ten poor men, who had to be members of the Holy Trinity Guild, and a woman to act as housekeeper for them. Although the basic structure of the building is unchanged it suffered a long period of neglect which led to large-scale restoration in the nineteenth century. Inevitably, therefore, the present exterior bears little resemblance to the original, but it is still a very attractive building which forms part of a picturesque courtyard group with the adjacent Bablake School.

The building still offers homes to elderly people and in 1974 a new wing was added to provide ten more flats. The original building underwent further internal modernisation to bring it up to modern standards of comfort.

COVENTRY — CITY CENTRE

THE GODIVA CLOCK

> *Access:* The clock is high on a wall in Broadgate. A-Z 116 5B

The story of eleventh century Lady Godiva is a highly prized tradition in Coventry but there are several versions of the tale. The gist of it seems to be that Godiva was distressed by the heavy taxation imposed on the citizens by her husband, Earl Leofric. She begged him to reduce the burden and he agreed to do so if she would ride naked through the streets. This she did, with her long hair strategically arranged, and Leofric honoured his promise.

The event is commemorated by a puppet clock which dates from Coventry's post-war reconstruction. When the clock strikes the hour the doors slide open and Godiva rides once again, while Peeping Tom leers down at her from above. At least, that's what is supposed to happen, but the clock has had a chequered career. There have been occasions when the doors have opened and closed a dozen times without any appearance by Godiva; conversely, the wayward lady has sometimes made up to twenty consecutive rides. And a former Lord Mayor probably recalls with embarrassment the day he waited with a party of visitors for Godiva to appear, only for the opening doors to reveal nothing more than a pair of pigeons.

These days the mechanism is more reliable and the clock works smoothly enough. Opinions may be divided about its aesthetic appeal but tourists seem to like it and coaches have been known to repeatedly circle Broadgate at a snail's pace, waiting for Godiva to appear.

COVENTRY — CITY CENTRE

PEEPING TOM

> *Access:* On the first floor of Cathedral Lanes Shopping Centre, Broadgate. A-Z 116 5B

The story of Godiva's ride may or may not be true but she herself certainly existed. Peeping Tom is another matter, an embellishment to the tale who didn't appear until the seventeenth century. The story goes that when Godiva made her bareback ride the citizens stayed indoors out of respect. A tailor called Tom, however, couldn't resist peeping from his window and was instantly struck blind in punishment. Although sheer invention, the phrase "Peeping Tom" has passed into common usage.

Tom never existed; nonetheless his statue does. Life-size, carved from oak and

wearing armour it probably came originally from a religious house and represents a warrior saint, either St George or St Michael. It was most likely made in the fifteenth century but by the eighteenth century saints were out of fashion and it became Peeping Tom instead.

Over the years Tom has moved around and by 1879 he was installed at the King's Head, in a specially built niche on the exterior wall, from which he gazed out over Hertford Street. During the war he was put into safe storage then later moved to the lobby of the Hotel Leofric. In 1990 he passed to St Martin's Property Corporation. Now, from the first floor of the shopping centre - surely the ultimate humiliation - against a background of shell suits and trainers, he looks down once more on Godiva, whose statue stands below. Poor Tom, imprisoned in a glass case and distractingly lit by spotlights, how he must yearn for the good old days in the fresh air outside the King's Head!

COVENTRY — CITY CENTRE

THE ELEPHANT AND CASTLE

> *Access:* In Broadgate, outside Cathedral Lanes. A-Z 116 5B

This particular elephant and castle is just one example of a motif which is repeated all over Coventry. While it's fun to go elephant hunting in this unlikely setting it does make you wonder what an elephant carrying a castle has to do with a Midlands city.

The elephant and castle is actually the main feature of Coventry's modern coat of arms, along with the eagle of Leofric and a phoenix symbolising the rebirth of the city from the ashes of wartime destruction. The oldest Coventry Seal in existence, which dates back to the thirteenth century, also has the elephant and castle motif, although this elephant stands by an oak tree and shares the crest with a dragon-slaying St Michael.

In the very first natural history books, known as bestiaries, animals were given religious associations. One such book contains a story of a sleeping elephant leaning against a tree which is being felled by hunters. The elephant crashes to the ground but is saved by a baby elephant which hauls him to his feet. According to historian Mary Dormer Harris, this story suggested to our medieval ancestors the Fall of Adam and Eve and Christ's redemption of the human race.

A different version portrays the elephant as a dragon-slayer, with the dragon as the counterpart of the Eden serpent. This provides a connection with St Michael, who also features on the early Seal. An even more famous dragon-slayer is St George and, oddly enough, Coventry is often supposed to have been his birthplace.

But it doesn't explain the castle does it? In fact, most medieval pictures of elephants include the castle, and nobody really knows why. One idea is that the elephant was seen as a beast so strong he could carry a castle full of soldiers, thus preserving them from defeat; by implication, this preserves the city too. Another suggestion is that an elephant carrying a castle is unable to bend his knee, thus symbolising civic pride. A third explanation which has often been proposed concerns the Black Prince, who owned a local manor. His wife was the Infanta of Castile, and it's easy to imagine this being corrupted to elephant and castle. Moreover, it seems that the Prince also owned that area of London known as the Elephant and Castle. It fits beautifully - until you remember that the thirteenth century Coventry Seal depicting an elephant and castle actually pre-dates the Prince and his Infanta by many years!

Elephant and Castle

COVENTRY — CITY CENTRE

THE STARLEY MEMORIAL

> *Access*:   On Greyfriars Green by Warwick Row. A-Z 116 5B

This monument to James Starley is rather out of the way and goes largely unnoticed, but Starley is an important part of Coventry's story; the man who turned a depressed town into the centre of the cycle industry.

In the 1860's, student Rowley Turner was so impressed by the velocipede, a prototype cycle then fashionable in Paris, that he brought one over to Coventry in the hope that his uncle, Josiah Turner, of the Coventry Sewing Machine Company, would agree to make velos as well. CSMC became Coventry Machinists, and the inventive company foreman, James Starley, who had been busy developing ever improved sewing machines, jumped at this new challenge.

The timing was perfect thanks to the Franco-Prussian War - a setback for the French industry but a blessing for Coventry which rapidly became a leader in the field. Cycles improved by leaps and bounds, largely due to innovations developed by Starley, and cycling became hugely popular. Suddenly Coventry was a boom town, the cycle capital of the world.

Together with another company employee, William Hillman, Starley developed a lightweight penny farthing in 1870. They called it the Ariel and, as a publicity stunt, embarked on a ride to London which took from dawn to midnight and so exhausted the pair that they were days in bed recovering.

Other inventions included the differential gear, the idea for which came to Starley as he lay in a ditch after an accident on a four-wheeler which he had been riding with his son who, younger and stronger, had been out-pedalling him, causing the machine to overturn.

Starley's most famous invention was a tricycle which he named the Salvo. Queen Victoria ordered two for the Royal household and Starley was asked to demonstrate its use to the Queen. For this he received a gold watch and the trike was henceforth known as the Royal Salvo.

On James Starley's death the city's cycle factories closed down so that workers could attend his funeral, and a fund was started which resulted in the erection of the memorial three years later. It is not a statue of the man himself but a portrayal of Fame; Starley is commemorated only by a medallion portrait and by mention of some of his inventions. Sadly, the memorial has been damaged by vandals - Fame has lost an arm and Starley his nose.

His sons carried on their father's work, introducing yet more innovations. Ironically, the motor trade developed directly from the cycle trade and, as the former grew, so the latter declined.

The Starley Memorial

HAWKESBURY

HAWKESBURY JUNCTION also known as SUTTON STOP

> *Access:* On the Warwickshire border 3½ miles north east of Coventry city centre and 1 mile east of M6 junction 3. Off Grange Road. A-Z 101 2F

Hawkesbury Junction is a great place both for industrial archaeologists and for gongoozlers - those who enjoy watching the canal scene from dry land. The Oxford and Coventry canals meet here and in times past it was well known as a lively place with long queues of working boats waiting to negotiate the locks, a Salvation Army mission boat to look after needy canal families and some pretty action-packed evenings at the Greyhound Inn! But that was in the days of commercial traffic and hard-living, hard- drinking boatmen and it's a very different place today. In 1976 it was designated a conservation area and the British Waterways Board undertook substantial restoration work which won a major environmental award.

The old atmosphere went with the narrowboatmen, despite a new generation of leisure users, but at least the junction is a cleaner, healthier and safer place and a remarkable array of canal artefacts survives. These include the shell of an engine house which once contained one of Thomas Newcomen's steam pumping engines, an attractive row of cottages, a chandlery, a former boatyard, a gentrified but very useful version of the old rough, tough Greyhound, the former toll clerk's office and several bridges, of which the best is a superb cast iron roving bridge made at Derby's Britannia Foundry in 1837. There are locks too, of course, and an unusual feature of the stop lock is that it has a rise of less than 7", probably the result of a surveying error by James Brindley, or by his clerk of works. The actual junction of the two canals almost looks like a mistake too, because it involves boat users navigating the most incredibly acute bend. Gongoozlers enjoy watching the novices on this one!

RADFORD

CASH'S TOPSHOPS

> *Access:* On Cash's Lane, off Foleshill Road 1 mile north of the city centre.
> A-Z 116 2B

Coventry has a long history of textile manufacture. By the nineteenth century many citizens were employed in the traditional cottage industry of weaving. But the introduction of the power loom meant the beginning of the end for weaving as a cottage industry and resentful workers vented their feelings in riots and machine-breaking.

Industrialist Joseph Cash thought he had the solution and he planned an ambitious scheme to help maintain the independence of the individual workers within a centralised system, at the same time removing the need for them to walk often long distances to work. In 1857 he built terraces of three-storey brick houses which incorporated living quarters on the lower floors and workshops, lit by oversized windows, on the top floor. For the occupants of Cash's Topshops going to work was now a simple matter of climbing through a trap door - but it can't have been much fun for those below, forced to listen to the interminable crashing of heavy looms overhead.

The Topshops were also known as the Hundred Houses as a hundred were planned originally, although only forty-eight materialised. Competition from France hit Coventry manufacturers badly and by 1862 the Topshop workshops had been made into one factory to increase productivity.

Cash's has since moved into new premises and the Topshops refurbished as attractive canal-side flats. The company is still very much in business; it provided the ribbons for the ill-fated Royal Wedding in 1981, and it makes the name tapes which generations of mothers all over the world have sewn into their children's school uniforms.

BERKSWELL

CHURCH OF ST JOHN THE BAPTIST: THE PRIEST'S ROOM

Access: Berkswell is 5 miles west of Coventry and St John's Church is on Church Lane in the village centre. A-Z 112 4D

Berkswell is an attractive village with cottages grouped around a green. The church lies nearby, next to a beautiful seventeenth century house which was once the rectory. Pevsner calls St John's "easily the most interesting Norman village church in Warwickshire" and what was Warwickshire's loss in 1974 is certainly West Midlands's gain. Its most obvious feature of interest also gives it an extremely picturesque quality; this is a two-storeyed, timber-framed porch with fine oak arcading on the ground floor and close-set studding above, all set beneath a steeply pitched, tiled roof.

The upper floor originally served as a priest's room and was, at that time, reached by an exterior staircase. Later it was used as the village meeting house and a bench still runs around the interior wall, with pegs some distance above it on which the men would hang their hats. Today it is used as a vestry by the rector and churchwardens but it is open to the public and contains many items of interest.

The porch was probably built in the late sixteenth century, or the early seventeenth; parish records show that repair work was carried out in 1611. The lead-lighted windows are the original ones and the key, which is still in daily use, was made in 1612.

BERKSWELL

CHURCH OF ST JOHN THE BAPTIST: THE CRYPT

The crypt is entered from stairs hidden by a pew in the north aisle, and is an extremely fine example of Norman architecture; very few English churches possess such a treasure. It was built in two parts, the eastern one in about 1150, the octagonal western part some years later. However, a major restoration in 1968 revealed part of an earlier wall thought to be late eighth century, so it seems that the Normans rebuilt a much earlier Saxon crypt. Part of these early walls can be seen, protected by a glass panel. Other items of interest include a thirteenth century coffin lid and a low stone bench which runs around the walls; such a facility was commonly provided for the use of children and the elderly, giving rise to the saying "the weakest go to the wall".

But why should a small village church possess such a crypt? It may have been to house the remains of some Saxon saint. The Tudor historian Leland claimed that St Milred, a Bishop of Worcester who died in 772, was buried here. Others have suggested instead St Mildred, Abbess of Minster-in-Thanet, who died in 725. Although she was buried at Minster and later moved to Canterbury it is possible that her kinsman, King Ethelbald of Mercia, may have obtained a relic with which to endow Berkswell. Perhaps he was baptised at the well and wished to show his gratitude. Relics provided an income for they attracted pilgrims. However, if this ever was a shrine to a saint he or she can't have been in great demand as the steps down to the crypt show very little wear.

BERKSWELL

CHURCH OF ST JOHN THE BAPTIST: CHURCH MICE

St John's contains a great deal of twentieth century woodwork, including the sanctuary chairs, the pulpit and the font. It is rare for a font to be made from wood but this one is carved from solid oak and was given in memory of a former rector's son, lost at sea in World War Two. It carries a motif of vine leaves inspired by those on the ancient screens which still survive in the nave. The man responsible for this woodwork was the renowned Robert Thompson of Kilburn in Yorkshire. If you look closely at the font you will find Thompson's trademark, a life-size mouse which he carved on each piece he made. Altogether, there are eleven such mice in Berkswell church - can you find them all?

Berkswell Church: Robert Thompson's Mouse.

BERKSWELL

THE WELL

> *Access:* On Church Lane by the village green.

Berkswell Church is not dedicated to St John the Baptist by chance. The village originated as a clearing in the Forest of Arden where a group of monks from Lichfield set up a small settlement by a spring or well which took its name from Bercol, either its discoverer or its owner. Bercol's Well eventually became Berkswell, of course, but long before it did the monks would have been busy baptising their converts in the well and it is often suggested that King Ethelbald of Mercia was himself baptised here.

The well was used for complete immersion baptism and is a 16' square, sunken, stone-walled structure entered by brick and stone steps. A notice indicates that it was restored by subscription in 1851 and another one informs that it is an offence to let dogs bathe in it. Sadly, they would have difficulty in doing so anyway, for at the time of writing (late 1992) the well is dry, despite weeks of heavy rain.

BERKSWELL

THE BEAR INN: A CANNON AND A PUMP

Access: On Spencer's Lane, by the crossroads in the village centre.

The Bear Inn is a most attractive, sixteenth century, timber- framed pub which used to be named the Bear and Ragged Staff after the emblem of the Earls of Warwick. Although it has shortened its name, a bear still climbs a ragged staff in the car park. Outside the front of the building is a cannon captured in the Crimean War by a Captain Arthur E Wilmot. An inscription reads:-

> *This Russian gun captured in the Crimean War in 1858 was brought home in triumph and ceremoniously "planted" outside this Inn. To mark the occasion the gun was fired at one o'clock and a celebration dinner was held in the Bear, on January 4th 1859.*

The local gentry paid 3s 6d each to attend the dinner, a sum which wouldn't buy you so much as a bag of peanuts at the bar today! By all accounts, however, the Bear still does good meals.

A few yards away, on the street corner, stands an unusual wooden pump with a stone sink at its base. The sink is obviously not in its original position because it's below the handle, not the spout. Such timber pumps are rare, but there is a similar one in Bayley Lane, Coventry, dated 1851.

BERKSWELL

THE STOCKS

Access: On the village green.

The stocks at Berkswell are famous; almost every book about West Midlands or the old county of Warwickshire gives them a mention and so do many books which cover the country as a whole. Naturally, you end up with the impression that these are something special, and you wonder why there's never a photograph of them. So this book is going to set the record straight and warn you not to expect too much! Berkswell's stocks have been caged in a ridiculous fenced enclosure which hugs them so tightly you can hardly see them. It enhances neither the stocks nor their setting, and we can only hope it's temporary. It certainly explains the lack of photos; the skill of a contortionist was the main requirement in obtaining the one here.

This strange treatment aside, the stocks are of intrinsic interest in that they have five holes instead of the conventional two or four. It has been suggested that there were once six holes but when one end rotted it was cut off, taking the sixth hole with it. But the remaining timber is perfectly sound; would one small part succumb so completely to rot that it had to be removed? An alternative explanation is more appealing - it claims that the stocks were made especially to accommodate a particularly troublesome one-legged offender and his two sidekicks.

ELMDON

THE MAGLEV

> *Access:* Birmingham International Airport and Birmingham International Railway Station. Both are on the A45 Coventry Road by M42 J6. A-Z 94 3C

Since its new terminal building was opened in the mid-1980's Birmingham Airport has become the fifth busiest airport in the UK, and is a major centre for both holiday and business flights. In 1984 it was linked to the National Exhibition Centre and Birmingham International Railway Station by yet another Brummie "first" - a revolutionary "train" which works on the principle of magnetic levitation and has no wheels. This light transit system is known as the Maglev and it operates a shuttle service which can transport over forty passengers from rail station to airport in ninety seconds.

HAMPTON-IN-ARDEN

CHURCH OF ST MARY AND ST BARTHOLOMEW: A HEART TOMB

> *Access:* On the corner of High Street and Solihull Road. Hampton is about 3½ miles north east of Solihull. A-Z 111 2E

Hampton is the traditional centre of the Forest of Arden, now long gone, and the setting of Shakespeare's "As You Like It". The most interesting building is the church, which has an unusual semi-circular stair turret on its tower. There are many other features of interest, including some lovely modern windows by two Midlands ladies, Elsie Whitford and Norah Yoxhall.

Most intriguing, however, is what is thought to be a heart tomb in the chancel. This consists of a moulded canopy surrounding a trefoiled arch in which a kneeling figure holds a shield. So- called heart tombs came into fashion during the First Crusade when it was impractical to bring bodies home for burial; hearts, however, were another matter. Quite a few found their way home, often being bequeathed to a friend, or to a favourite church. They were usually enclosed in precious metals, but lead caskets were also used, and the practice continued for centuries, although few tombs have survived.

During restoration work the wall was opened up and a small leaden box was found behind the carving. Nothing remained inside but it certainly favoured the heart tomb theory. It may be that the heart was that of a Knight Templar from Temple Balsall, killed in the Holy Land about 1190. We shall never know.

To the west of the church, Moat House still shows traces of its twelfth century origins and is said to have once belonged to an ancestor of Shakespeare's mother.

KNOWLE

CHURCH OF ST JOHN BAPTIST, ST LAWRENCE AND ST ANNE: STRANDED SEDILIA

> *Access:* At the junction of High Street and Kenilworth Road. Knowle is 2½ miles south east of Solihull. A-Z 126 3B

Built in the Perpendicular style, and consecrated in 1402, Knowle church contains a great deal of fine carving, including some appealing misericords and a marvellous rood screen. A curious feature of the chancel, however,is the row of stone seats (sedilia) marooned half-way up the wall, well out of reach of anyone wishing to sit down.

Such seats are often found in churches, but usually in a more practical position! They were intended for the use of the minister and those assisting him at communion services. What went wrong at Knowle is that the church was extended in 1412 and this either took it up against a building which was in the way, or it took it to the boundary of its land. Either way, this left no room for processions to walk around the building and, as processional was an important part of the Medieval Church, a solution had to be found. This took the form of a subway under the church, which necessitated the raising of the floor level in the chancel. The sedilia date from this time and served their purpose for over 300 years.

In the eighteenth century it was discovered that the subway was threatening the stability of the building and so it was filled in; the blocked-up entrance is still visible outside. This meant the floor level could be restored to its original position - but the sedilia were left stranded.

MERIDEN

THE CENTRE OF ENGLAND

> *Access:* On Meriden Green. Meriden is 5 miles west of Coventry, off the A45.
> A-Z 96 5C

Meriden is a village of ancient origins but many of its old houses have now gone, while new ones have sprung up to house commuters. Much of interest survives, however, and at the western end of the village green is the headless shaft of an old cross, carved from weathered pink sandstone, delicately stained with mosses and lichens. An inscription reads:-

> *This ancient wayside cross has stood in the village for some 500 years and by tradition it marks the Centre of England. The cross was rebuilt on this site when the green was improved in celebration of the Festival of Britain AD 1951.*

Behind the cross, a shop also bears the legend "The Centre of England", and the nearby Bull's Head has a brass plate set into the floor, again affirming the tradition.

Many consider it a dubious claim and, in fact, there are rivals, all of them in Warwickshire (as was Meriden until 1974). One of these, Lillington, marks the spot with an oak tree. Celia Fiennes, travelling in the 1690's, wrote "I came to High Cross which is esteemed the middle of England". High Cross is about 20 miles east of Meriden and was an important Roman crossroads, the place where Watling Street was intersected by the Fosse Way.

In truth, there are as many "centres of England" as there are criteria for calculating it, but Meriden has staked its claim with more determination than most, and it seems as good a place as any.

TEMPLE BALSALL

THE CHURCH OF ST MARY, THE OLD HALL AND LADY KATHERINE'S HOSPITAL

> *Access:* Temple Balsall is between Knowle and Balsall Common on the B4101.
> A-Z 127 4F

Temple Balsall is a tiny community which has developed from an estate of the Knights Templar, an order of warrior monks founded in 1118 to protect pilgrims in the Holy Land. Their work was largely financed by gifts from the aristocracy which often took the form of land. This was the case at Balsall which was given by Roger de Mowbray, probably in 1146. A thriving farm was established and in the thirteenth century the Old Hall was built, as was St Mary's church, replacing an earlier chapel.

The Templars did not always live up to their high ideals and, in any case, their increasing wealth inevitably led to envy. In 1308 the order was forcibly disbanded and its estates given to a similar organisation, the Knights Hospitaller. Little is known about the Hospitallers at Temple Balsall but from 1470 the property was leased to a succession of lay tenants until seized by Henry VIII at the Dissolution of the Monasteries. In later years it passed to Elizabeth I's favourite, Robert Dudley, and then to his grand-daughters Lady Anne Holbourne and Lady Katherine Leveson.

The Templars' church had fallen into ruin but Lady Anne paid for its restoration while Lady Katherine endowed a hospital (almshouse) for twenty poor women and a free school for twenty poor boys. The minister of the church was also to serve as schoolteacher and master of the hospital and a house was provided for him. Lady Katherine set up a board of trustees and their successors still administer the charity today.

The hospital buildings face each other across a courtyard, with the master's house forming the third side of the group. The ladies used to walk each day along the footpath to the Old Hall - built by the Templars and later the home of the bailiff - to collect their bread ration and the path is still known as the Breadwalk. By 1736 the Old Hall was in a poor state of repair and was replaced by Temple House which stands opposite the church. Later, the remains of the Old Hall were turned into cottages for the sexton and the curate, and these still stand next to the church.

St Mary's was restored by Sir George Gilbert Scott in 1864 and the schoolroom was replaced around the same time. The hospital has recently been refurbished to provide modern flats and is now open to men as well as women.

Temple Balsall

WALSALL

CHURCH OF ST MATTHEW: A MYSTERY TUNNEL

> *Access:*   On Church Hill in the town centre. A-Z 33 2H

Walsall's fine thirteenth century church stands high above the town on 500'
Church Hill, a prominent landmark for miles around. There are some interesting
misericords inside but the church is only very rarely open - except, of course, for
services. But you don't need to go inside to appreciate St Matthew's most unusual
feature - an arched tunnel which runs underneath the chancel. It may be, as at
Knowle, that when the church was extended it left no room for processions to
walk round it and so the tunnel was built to solve the problem. There is a local
tradition, however, that the church lay in the path of a proposed road to
Birmingham and the tunnel was constructed to take the road under it. This seems
unlikely - why not simply go round?

Such explanations assume that the church was altered at some stage - but could it
have been built this way initially? The Hereford man, Alfred Watkins, who came
up with the theory of ley lines (published in 1925 in "The Old Straight Track")
claimed there were several instances of churches actually being built deliberately
on ancient tracks, with tunnels or doorways provided for travellers to pass
through. He sites examples at Warwick and Exeter, and it seems that the same is
true of Holy Trinity in Coventry. A number of churches have blocked-up
archways or doorways which are not always so easy to account for as the one at
Knowle.

WALSALL

SISTER DORA

Access: At The Bridge - the junction of Bridge Street and Digbeth in the town centre. A-Z 33 2H

The statue of Sister Dora was erected in 1886, the first in Britain of a woman other than Royalty, and a mark of the great love felt for Dora by the people of Walsall. Born Dorothy Wyndlow Pattison in Yorkshire, in 1832, she was in her thirties when she joined the Sisterhood of the Good Samaritan to train as a nurse. Walsall Corporation had asked the Sisters to open a hospital for the victims of industrial accidents and when the Sister-in-charge fell ill in 1865 Dora was thrown into the breach, despite having practically no experience. For the next thirteen years she devoted her life to the care of the sick and needy, coping with endless smallpox epidemics, as well as the victims of colliery disasters, blast furnace explosions and all manner of horrific accidents. She eventually left the Sisterhood and took charge of a hospital where she was soon successfully performing minor operations. A pioneer in her field, her ceaseless courage, care and compassion made her a household name in the town. She achieved national status too, when Walsall Cottage Hospital was declared to be the most efficiently run in the country.

Dora's death in 1878 was due to cancer but until the very end she continued her work on the wards, always cheerful and smiling, so that none guessed at her suffering. When she died thousands mourned and her name is still honoured today.

Unfortunately, Walsall's pigeons are fond of her too, as you can see from the photograph, and the Council does not appreciate the constant battle to keep poor Dora clean!

WOLVERHAMPTON

CHURCH OF ST PETER: STONE PULPIT

Access: Set back from Lichfield Street to the north of the main shopping area.
A-Z 29 1H

St Peter's Collegiate Church is a fine thirteenth-century building which stands
behind pleasant gardens at the highest point of Wolverhampton on the site where
the town's first church was built in about 994 AD by the Lady Wulfruna. There is
much to admire inside but the outstanding feature is a rare stone pulpit reached
by a staircase attached to one of the pillars in the nave. The whole structure is

beautifully made and
perfectly preserved, and
is graced by the notable
addition of a carved lion
crouching on the
balustrade. There is a
tradition among St
Peter's choirboys that the
lion yawns when a
sermon goes on too
long. The pulpit dates
from the fifteenth
century and bears the
coat of arms of
Humphrey Swinerton of
Hilton who gave it to the
church.

Also of great interest are
the fifteenth-century
font, beautifully carved
with the figures of
various saints, and the
tomb of Colonel John
Lane of Bentley who,
together with his
daughter Jane, was
principally responsible
for organising the escape
from England of Charles
II after his defeat at the
Battle of Worcester in
1651.

CHURCH OF ST PETER: SAXON PILLAR

> *Access:*   Outside the church in St Peter's Gardens.

Probably the oldest man-made object to survive in Wolverhampton is a 14ft-high circular pillar standing outside St Peter's. It is usually referred to as a preaching cross but only the shaft remains. Such crosses were used to mark a preaching place in the days before the community could afford to build a church. This is one of the largest and most impressive of its kind and is covered with carvings of birds and animals in typically lively Saxon style. The carvings are about a thousand years old but the shaft itself may be nearer two thousand as it is possible it was taken from the Roman town of Wroxeter, about 25 miles away.

There is no firm evidence of this, however.

Sadly, the pillar is seriously eroded and blackened - the past two hundred years of pollution probably having had more effect than a thousand years of mere weathering. Acid rain will continue to eat away at it over the years and it's fortunate that casts were taken of the carvings in 1877. These are now in the Victoria and Albert Museum; at least future generations will have some idea of how the shaft once looked, but it's a poor substitute for the real thing.

WOLVERHAMPTON

CHURCH OF ST PETER: THE BARGAIN STONE

Access: Outside the church.

Not far from the Saxon pillar stands a strange stone about a yard high, rather like a curved headstone except that it has a round hole punched through it near the top. Tradition says that in the days before written contracts were necessary Wolverhampton traders would seal bargains or exchanges by clasping hands through the hole.

WOLVERHAMPTON

GIFFARD HOUSE AND THE CHURCH OF ST PETER AND ST PAUL

> *Access:*   On North Street behind the Civic Centre. A-Z 29 1H

Stranded between the ring road and the hideous modern Civic Centre is an elegant three-storey, five-bay house of mellow Georgian brick built 1726-33 for the Giffards, a Roman Catholic family from Chillington, near Penk, in Staffordshire. A small chapel for holding Mass was incorporated into the building - the first post-reformation Catholic church in Britain. The chapel was enlarged in 1765 and by 1804 it had become the headquarters of the Catholic church in the Midlands. Bishop John Milner, who played a major role in the process of Catholic emancipation, was resident here until his death in 1826. In 1825 a substantial church was actually built onto Giffard House, incorporating the earlier chapel. With its elegant stuccoed exterior, and fine classical interior, this is one of the most impressive churches in Wolverhampton, and certainly the most unusual.

WOLVERHAMPTON

W T M SNAPE

Access: On Queen Street in the town centre. A-Z 29 1H

Queen Street is, architecturally speaking, probably the best street in Wolverhampton, with a number of very impressive buildings, including the superb County Court. Snape's, at number 27, is not particularly smart, but the slightly shabby exterior of this tea and coffee merchant's hides a fascinating interior. Dating back to the 1830's this is the oldest shop in town and many of the original fittings survive.

The window display hints at what is to come, with its row of old- fashioned globe lamps, oriental prints, figurines and caddies, brass trays and porcelain dishes of tea and coffee. Inside, you return to a more gracious era as you admire the mahogany counter with its old brass scales, black and gold tea canisters emblazoned with dragons and other eastern designs, and the tools of the trade suspended from the ceiling on a pulley. It comes almost as a bonus that you can purchase a wide variety of fragrant teas and freshly-ground coffees in both traditional and modern blends. All shops should be like this!

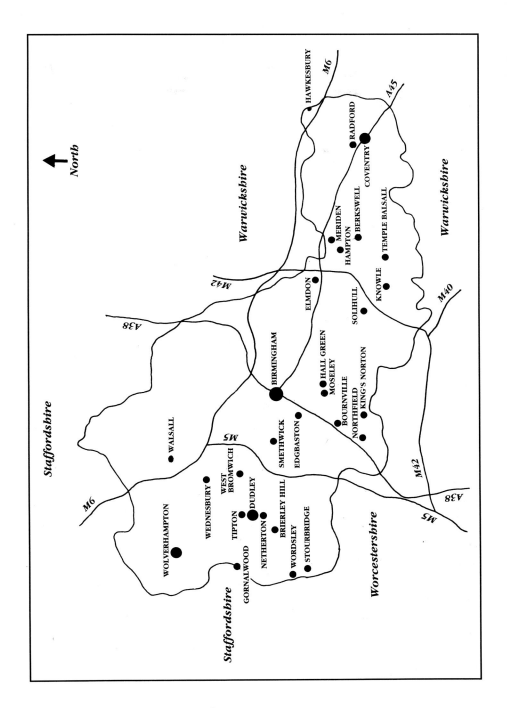

BIBLIOGRAPHY

Bird Vivian, *Staffordshire*
Bird Vivian, *Portrait of Birmingham*
Bird Vivian, *Exploring the West Midlands*
Bird Vivian, *Streetwise*
Burton Anthony, *The Shell Book of Curious Britain*
Burton Anthony and Coote Clive, *Industrial Archaeological Sites of Britain*
Falconer Keith, *Guide to England's Industrial Heritage*
Groves Peter, *Exploring Birmingham*
Hickman Douglas, *Warwickshire*
Hillier Caroline, *A Journey to the Heart of England*
Little Bryan, *Birmingham Buildings - The Archaeological Story of a Midlands City*
Mee Arthur, *The King's England - Staffordshire*
Mee Arthur, *The King's England - Warwickshire*
Newbold E B, *Portrait of Coventry*
Parker Mike, *The Raw Guide to Birmingham and the Black Country*
Parsons Harold, *Portrait of the Black Country*
Pearson J R G, *Along the Birmingham Canals - A Boating and Walking Guide*
Pearson Michael, *Canal Companion - Birmingham Canal Navigations*
Pearson Michael, *Canal Companion - South Midlands and Warwickshire Ring*
Pevsner Nikolaus, *The Buildings of England - Staffordshire*
Pevsner Nikolaus, *The Buildings of England - Worcestershire*
Pevsner Nikolaus and Wedgwood Alexandra, *The Buildings of England - Warwickshire*
Shirley Peter, *Wildlife Walkabouts - Birmingham and the Black Country*
Shirley Peter, *West Midlands Countryside*
Skipp Victor, *The Centre of England*
Thorold Henry, *Staffordshire*
Timpson John, *Timpson's Towns of England and Wales - Oddities and Curiosities*
Timpson John, *Timpson's England - a Look Beyond the Obvious*
West Midlands Federation of Women's Institutes, *The West Midlands Village Book*
Zuckerman Joan and Eley Geoffrey, *Birmingham Heritage*

INDEX

S.B. Publications publish other titles in this series of county curiosities.
For details write (enclosing SAE) to:–
S.B. Publications, c/o 19 Grove Road, Seaford, East Sussex BN25 1TP.